Contents

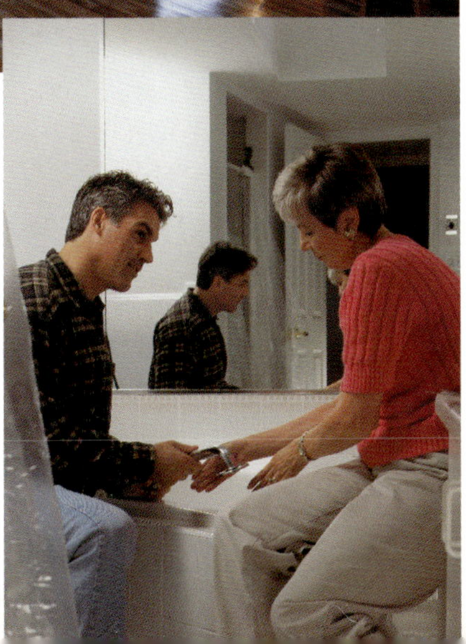

Cover: The wood inlay floor of this family room adds dimension and design to the space in the same way as a throw rug. Find out more about this home built by Minto Developments of Ottawa and Toronto on page 52.

Housing of the future—Why

It's a simple fact. Life does not stand still. People age, families change, and so do their needs—especially when it comes to living space. FlexHousing is a new and innovative approach to home design, renovation and construction, able to adapt and convert affordably as people's lifestyles change. This practical and modern-day approach to and affordability are the basic principles of FlexHousing. The best FlexHousing design also includes the principles of Healthy Housing: occupant health, energy and resource efficiency, and designs built to endure. FlexHousing makes sense for those who want to create beautiful, practical housing that meets today's needs.

FlexHousing brings together the best of everything

designing and building housing of all kinds—from single-family dwellings to duplexes, multi-units, townhouses and even apartments—allows residents to convert space to meet their changing needs. Imagine housing that is planned for subdividing rooms, expanding space or converting attics and garages into bedrooms, family rooms, home offices or self-contained suites.

FlexHousing brings together the best of everything we know about building houses and living in them. Adaptability, accessibility

In Canada, the United States and Europe, this new approach to home design and building is giving homeowners more flexible living space than ever before. Designed and pre-engineered to adapt to the changing needs of its occupants over their lifetimes, FlexHousing is housing of the future, available today.

FlexHousing means homeowners no longer have to move simply to get another bathroom or more living space. Need to convert a family room into two bedrooms? With a FlexHouse, it's no problem because the rooms are designed and built for change, complete with pre-wiring. Will your parents be moving in with you someday? A FlexHouse can give them their own suite of rooms, where they can live in comfort and privacy, yet always be close.

That's the beauty of FlexHousing. It allows your home to change or expand without costly and inconvenient renovations. Like a true friend, a house designed according to FlexHousing principles grows with you.

FlexHousing?

by Tom Parker
Tom Parker, a CMHC researcher, is the FlexHousing project manager.

Comfort and convenience

Most homes built in Canada in the last 50 years are for two-parent families with two or more children. Kitchens and bathrooms are usually small with narrow doorways, making them inaccessible to anyone with mobility problems. It can be difficult and expensive to adapt these houses to take advantage of new housing technology—advances that can improve quality of life and save money through energy efficiency. Housing that meets Canadians' needs in the 21st century will respond to the wave of change engulfing us by being adaptable to the needs of people at every stage of life.

we know about building houses and living in them.

FlexHousing offers people more choice in housing.

FlexHousing meets the needs of its occupants, whether they are single, traditional families, single-parent families, multi-generation families, empty nesters or simply friends living together. On the outside, it looks no different than conventional housing. On the inside, many of its features are barely visible. Yet this type of housing improves its occupants' quality of life by bringing together spacious, barrier-free design with adaptable, convertible space. Combining FlexHousing principles with the latest in housing technology, healthy materials and improved indoor air ventilation systems creates more comfortable and convenient living space, and helps protect occupants' health and the natural environment.

FlexHousing applies to any kind of new housing construction—from singles and duplexes to multi-unit condominiums and apartments; it also works in renovation projects. Referred to as Universal Housing in the United States and Lifetime Homes in the United Kingdom, FlexHousing offers more people more choice in housing than ever before and addresses the key housing challenges of a changing world.

Tom Parker

Changing *with the* times

The house of the future

How will Canadians live in the 21st century? What will our cities and homes be like? While no one has a crystal ball, futurists and researchers are sure of one thing: change will be constant, and it will affect everything. The advance of technology and the changing nature of work, commerce, entertainment and education, as well as the aging of the population and the changing structure of the Canadian family, mean a greater variety of lifestyles and living arrangements.

The housing needs of Canadians will also change, and Canada's houses will have to change in response. Demographic shifts, lifestyle trends and new technologies will have a tremendous effect on housing demand, not only on the number of houses built, bought and sold, but on the quality of the houses themselves.

FlexHousing takes the best of everything in housing today and puts it all under one roof.

The advance of technology and the changing nature of work, commerce, entertainment and education, as well as the aging of the population and the changing structure of the Canadian family, mean a greater variety of lifestyles and living arrangements.

Three main groups make up the housing market in Canada: the "pre-boomers," the "baby boomers" and the "post-boomers" or "Generation X."

On the home front today

Three main groups make up the housing market in Canada: the "pre-boomers," born between 1930 and 1945; the "baby boomers," born between 1946 and 1964; and the "post-boomers" or "Generation X," born between 1965 and 1973.

The baby boomers are aging. That means the population as a whole is getting older. By the year 2017, half of all Canadian households will be headed by people 55 years old and older. Many baby boomers will be single or couples whose children have moved out. With more older households and fewer households of young families, Canada's rate of population growth will likely decline. These factors will play a major role in determining the size, design and features of the type of housing Canadians demand.

Housing needs are changing. Many people now work from home using computers and fax machines to link with employers and clients. As a result, today's housing must provide the space and utilities for home offices.

Canadians are spending more time at home. Whatever the reason—work, more time with the family, or the enjoyment of electronic entertainment—

Community response

Ultimately, the qualities and characteristics of housing reflect the qualities and characteristics of society itself, and the success of concepts such as FlexHousing is determined by popular demand. As society continues to undergo transformations, such as the aging of the population and the tendency to spend more work and recreational time at home, homebuyers will increasingly demand FlexHousing features in their homes.

Changing design, renovation and construction regulations will enable the housing industry to respond to the market. The regulatory changes can range from allowing rental suites, in-law apartments and home offices to incorporating flexible, adaptable and accessible features within building code standards. The case studies that follow show how some cities have responded to the changing housing market.

Secondary suites in Vancouver

In Vancouver, until 1986, the creation of a secondary dwelling within a single-family home was against city bylaws. High housing costs and a shortage of affordable rental units, however, caused numerous homeowners to demand the right—or to proceed despite bylaws—to install such units in their homes. The city responded quickly with changes to its bylaws. Subject to requirements for minimum ceiling heights, parking facilities and upgrades of services, the amended bylaws permitted the creation of secondary units within residential homes. The number of units is limited to two, and indoor access between them is mandatory.

This allowance of what has become known as Convertible Housing—FlexHousing by another name—proved practical and economical for homeowners and renters alike. Because they are regulated, these suites provide safe and healthy rental housing in established neighbourhoods. They have also allowed seniors to live independently within their communities, remaining close to family and friends.

Population estimates for 1996 and projections for 2016

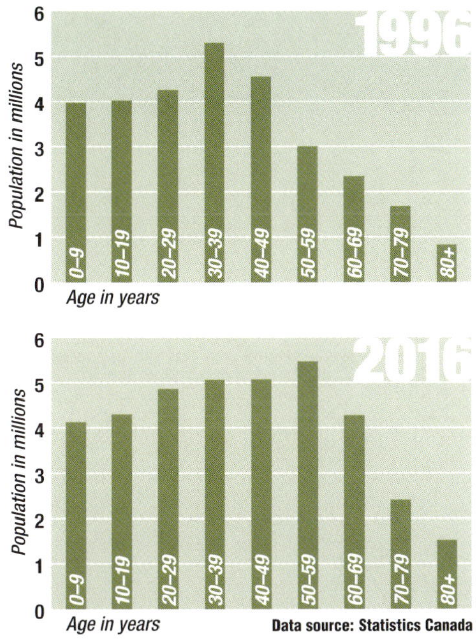

Data source: Statistics Canada

By 2016, 34 per cent of all Canadian households are expected to be non-family households.

people demand more comfort and convenience from their homes.

Space is another key issue for homeowners. People born at the end of the baby boom and post-boomers—along with renters, downtown residents and families with children—typically want to increase their living space by 30 per cent. On the other hand, pre-boomers and people born at the beginning of the baby boom are already looking for smaller houses that need less maintenance. As the baby boomers age, their preferences will likely follow the same course. Flexible living space is valuable to all.

For the most part, Canadians now 55 or older have a strong commitment to owning their own homes. They intend to remain in the homes they now own or move to smaller ones.

Many people now work from home using computers and fax machines to link with employers and clients. As a result, today's housing must provide the space and utilities for home offices.

Community response

Home offices in Markham

In many Canadian cities, bylaws seldom take into account workplaces in the home. In the late 1980s, Markham, Ontario, received a request from the Home-based Business Network to change its bylaws regarding home offices. After much research and consultation, a regulatory framework was developed. It was designed to have a positive effect on business owners and their surrounding communities. By dealing with issues such as parking, traffic, signage and noise, the new bylaws ensure that business owners can operate effectively out of their homes without disturbing their neighbours. There are several benefits to the municipality, including the encouragement of economic development; efficient land use; and control over the kinds of businesses established in its residential communities.

Canadians are spending more time at home.

Whatever the reason—work, more time with the family, or the enjoyment of electronic entertainment—people demand more comfort and convenience from their homes.

Most aging baby boomers, accustomed to independence and comfortable lifestyles, can be expected to have similar feelings. Indeed, as the baby boomers age, it will become increasingly important for housing to support self-sufficient, independent living because public institutions and governments may not have the resources to care for so many older people.

FlexHousing incorporates leading design and construction techniques to create living space that is adaptable, accessible, affordable and convertible.

Community response

Convenience for all in Britain

The aim of regulatory change is not to impose a model for housing on architects, builders or homebuyers. It is to make it easier to adopt housing that will be increasingly in demand and of benefit to everyone. Britain's recent decision to add elements of universal design to its national guidelines for new housing is an excellent example. Level entries, main-floor bathrooms and wider-than-usual doorways and halls are features that make housing more convenient for all. Such features are becoming increasingly necessary as the British population, like ours, grows older.

Housing for families in flux

A lower rate of population growth means fewer new households—and fewer new homes. The housing stock will age along with the population, ultimately affecting its overall quality and increasing the frequency of repairs and renovations.

FlexHousing, which is based on the best of everything in housing today, is ideal for replacing or renovating the housing stock. It incorporates leading design and construction techniques to create living space that is adaptable, accessible, affordable and convertible. It can also include healthy materials, ventilation systems and energy-efficient components. With all its adaptability, functional performance and energy efficiency, FlexHousing is built to endure because it meets the needs of the widest variety of people.

The renovation of older homes to include FlexHousing features can anticipate occupants' future needs. People looking for a house are more than twice as likely to buy a resale home as a new one. Upgrading with forward-looking, FlexHousing renovations will pay off by including features that bring convenience and comfort to as many people as possible.

Canada Mortgage and Housing Corporation predicts that the average size of the Canadian household will continue to shrink until the year 2016. At the same time, the number of non-family households (i.e., people living alone or with unrelated individuals) will increase faster than the number of family households. By 2016, 34 per cent of all Canadian households are expected to be non-family households.

In the coming years, as people's needs change, they will demand more versatility from housing. With fewer new homes being built, existing houses will need flexible features to accommodate different occupants' requirements easily and inexpensively. FlexHousing is a way of thinking about design, construction and renovation that offers homebuyers and occupants more choice, flexibility and convenience than conventional housing.

FlexHousing anticipates the day when renting a house, staying in one's own home as one grows older or becomes temporarily disabled, or accommodating a child with a disability will be that much easier because more and more homes will have this basic level of access.

Community response

Basic access in Austin

In Austin, Texas, legislation has made accessibility the law of the land for newly constructed single-family homes, duplexes and triplexes. A municipal ordinance requires that such housing incorporate minor adjustments in construction, including:

- one no-step entrance;
- all doors (including bathroom) at least 810 mm (32 in.) wide;
- halls and other rooms at least 910 mm (36 in.) wide;
- reinforcements in the bathroom walls around the toilet and bathtub or shower for installing grab-bars; and
- light switches and other environmental controls between 380 mm (15 in.) and 1,220 mm (48 in.) from the floor.

This ordinance improves basic access for people with disabilities. It also anticipates the day when renting a house, staying in one's own home as one grows older or becomes temporarily disabled, or accommodating a child with a disability will be that much easier because more and more homes will have this basic level of access.

Housing with four or more units (built after 1991) must meet a somewhat higher standard of accessibility under the U.S. *Fair Housing Amendments Act* of 1988. Housing with five or more units that received any federal financial assistance must meet the more stringent access requirements of the *Rehabilitation Act* of 1973.

FlexHousing is intelligent housing. It allows families to live longer in one place and communities to take root and grow. It provides a solution to the challenges of urban sprawl by presenting an infill-housing alternative that's clean, comfortable and modern. It can also promote the conservation of natural resources and incorporate energy-efficient systems that are healthier for homeowners. Instituting the principles of FlexHousing on the largest possible scale through building codes and other regulations will establish a firm foundation for the housing of tomorrow and raise the quality of life for everyone.

FlexHousing

What is it?

FlexHousing is the Canadian approach to a worldwide concern for creating homes that suit many different segments of the population. In other countries, similar approaches are called Universal Housing and Lifetime Homes. While the labels are different, these are houses designed and built to be adaptable. They provide living spaces made to evolve—easily and with minimum expense—to meet the changing needs of their occupants. The intentions are clear: to allow homeowners to occupy a dwelling for longer periods, to create dwellings that can meet a wide range of needs, and to improve the convenience a home can offer its occupants.

Whether it is FlexHousing, Universal Housing or Lifetime Homes, this design and building approach produces homes that adapt to the changing circumstances of the people who live in them while providing the highest levels of comfort, safety and efficiency.

Housing the world

Around the world, architects, researchers and urban planners are re-examining conventional approaches to housing. The purpose of housing—and the conditions affecting housing—are very different today than they were even 20 years ago.

For example, homes in a number of European countries tend to be built according to traditional design principles. But the needs of modern Europeans scarcely resemble those of previous generations. Researchers in Switzerland are attempting to reshape the way architects and builders think about housing.

In China, researchers are also developing dwellings that can be reconfigured easily and will comfortably house larger groups of people in densely populated cities.

In the United States, adaptable housing emphasizes accessibility—designs that can accommodate people at every stage of life—and barrier-free design—planning that can accommodate people with disabilities. After all, the American population, like Canada's, is getting older.

According to *Recent Research Results*, a newsletter of the U.S. Department of Housing and Urban Development, by the turn of the century, roughly one third of all Americans will be older than 65, disabled or chronically ill. The same article notes that fewer than one in 10 U.S. homes can meet the needs of this sizable population.

The United Kingdom is singularly advanced in adaptable housing. In March 1998, Britain's Parliament announced legislation requiring every new home to contain certain key design elements—many of which promote accessibility. These elements include an entrance with no steps, a main-floor bathroom and wider-than-usual doorways and halls. A long-time proponent of these measures, the U.K.'s Joseph Rowntree Foundation, developed Lifetime Homes. A concept similar to FlexHousing, Lifetime Homes are designed for accessibility, safety and sufficient adaptability to suit the changing requirements of their occupants.

Lifetime Homes in the United Kingdom fit every neighbourhood. (Joseph Rowntree Foundation)

The intentions are clear: to allow homeowners to occupy a dwelling for long periods, to create dwellings that can meet a wide range of needs, and to improve the convenience a home can offer its occupants.

The Rietveld-Schröder house, shown here and opposite, is an early example of inexpensive adaptable housing built in the Netherlands. (Central Museum Utrecht/Rietveld-Schröder Archive)

These affordable homes in Atlanta are examples of Universal Housing in the United States.

For one and all

One fundamental principle that gives FlexHousing universal appeal is that accessibility is not only an issue for older people or people with special needs. Everyone benefits from accessible homes. For example, an entry without steps is more convenient than one at the top of a flight of steps for both a person with a walker and a mother with a baby carriage. A bathroom with space beside the toilet and along the full length of the tub makes cleaning easier. Wider hallways make moving furniture a far less awkward task. And anyone who has ever broken a leg can appreciate a design that allows people to move around easily within the home. In fact, accessible housing is simply good design and common sense. No matter who you are, smart design makes life easier.

FlexHousing = choice

A great many features, fixtures, appliances and designs are associated with FlexHousing—from conveniently located electrical outlets to front-loading washers and ground-floor laundry rooms. It can also include elements of Healthy Housing, such as energy-efficient furnaces and improved indoor air ventilation systems that protect occupant well-being and the natural environment.

FlexHousing is not one particular kind of house. It is an approach to building homes using a range of design and construction refinements to create living space that is adaptable, accessible, affordable and convertible. Not all FlexHousing elements are meant for every home: the FlexHousing concept includes choice. Some people may find the idea of a ground-floor laundry room appealing, while others prefer that the same space be used for a second bathroom. Flex design could permit either possibility. Starting with one smart configuration, homeowners can change their houses into exactly what they want them to be.

This versatility makes FlexHousing a concept that can be applied to both renovations and new construction. With a little extra planning, many renovations provide excellent opportunities for incorporating flexible features. A kitchen renovation, for example, can include easy-to-reach, drop-down cupboards and new cabinets and countertops made in modules with large, easy-to-grip, D-shaped handles. These practical features are convenient for everyone, from young children to older people who have difficulty bending down or gripping small handles.

By making it possible for people to remain in their homes despite changes in their lives and personal needs, the concept contributes to neighbourhood stability, fostering a sense of community among residents.

Housing for life

Sooner or later, a growing family reaches the point at which yesterday's dream home becomes too small. Usually, there is just one choice: move to a bigger house. But moving can be difficult, disruptive and costly. Families find themselves leaving the neighbourhood they love; children have to switch schools and leave friends behind. Years later, when the children have grown up and the parents have retired, that second, larger home is too big and perhaps too difficult to maintain. The search for a new place then begins all over again.

In Canada, most homeowners prefer to stay where they are. FlexHousing allows homeowners to change their dwellings as their circumstances change. A large bedroom can easily and inexpensively be converted into two smaller, equally well-outfitted ones or a home office. An empty attic can become a master bedroom or a large family room, or an area of the basement can become a rental suite. As people grow older, FlexHousing's emphasis on accessibility makes the home easier to maintain and move around in while offering greater convenience, so occupants can live in the house longer.

Housing for the community

The advantages of FlexHousing are not limited to individual homeowners. By making it possible for people to remain in their homes despite changes in their lives and personal needs, the concept contributes to neighbourhood stability, fostering a sense of community among residents. It also increases security because long-time neighbours know and watch out for each other.

FlexHousing is ideal as high-quality single infill or townhouses, which can be made to fit easily into available city spaces. It allows municipalities to increase their population density without having to expand geographically, making more efficient use of urban infrastructure and creating a larger tax base.

FlexHousing is ideal as high-quality single infill or townhouses, which can be made to fit easily into available city spaces.

FlexHousing nailed down

FlexHousing is the housing solution for our changing society and for our changing needs as homeowners. It incorporates principles of design and construction that will satisfy the housing needs of Canadians in the 21st century. While almost countless features and systems exist to help put those principles into practice, not all are necessary for every housing project. That just wouldn't be flexible.

This Montreal townhouse can also be accessed through a rear grade-level entrance.

FlexHousing Features

ADAPTABLE

Adaptability means designing a home for several possible arrangements. Occupants can choose the arrangements that best meet their wants and needs. For example, the first floor of a FlexHouse can be designed for easy conversion to an apartment with full plumbing and a kitchenette—and the possibility of a private entrance. The upper floors can also serve as a self-contained home. Bathroom walls can be reinforced during construction for future installation of supportive fixtures such as grab-bars. Building such features into a new home can save time, money and trouble when changes to the living space are needed down the road.

With FlexHousing, prospective buyers get many homes in one. Through adaptable features such as convertible rooms and pre-designed external additions, occupants can create a home that's right for today and for tomorrow—without the troubles that conventional renovation can bring.

FlexHousing allows people to buy houses, apartments or condominiums that have the potential to adapt to their changing housing needs over time.

Bathroom walls can be reinforced during construction for future installation of supportive fixtures such as grab-bars.

In the end, the adaptable nature of FlexHousing makes it possible to create "housing for life." Rather than endure the problems of moving from place to place according to their changing needs, homeowners can change their homes' interior design and features, and continue to live in their homes in familiar comfort.

FlexHousing is housing built with the future in mind. It allows people to buy houses, apartments or condominiums that have the potential to adapt to their changing housing needs over time.

ADJUSTABLE FEATURES

Adaptability is achieved in part by including features that can adjust to meet homeowners' requirements. Adjustable features permit change without major renovation. Modular kitchen counters and cabinets, for example, can be adjusted vertically on brackets, or by inserting or removing extra sections below countertops.

A bathtub with free space along its entire length is less awkward to clean than one tucked in beside a toilet, and provides better access for everyone.

FlexHousing features add convenience and practicality to the functions of a home. A bathtub with free space along its entire length is less awkward to clean than one tucked in beside a toilet, and provides better access for everyone. Wider-than-usual doorways allow people to move furniture from one room to another without difficulty or to carry an armload of groceries into the kitchen without having to twist like a pretzel.

Accessibility and safety

In FlexHousing, reducing the potential danger of everyday household activities is a fundamental consideration. That's something everyone can appreciate, especially as the average age of the population increases. Smoke detectors are built into the design. Non-slip

The FlexHousing concept is user-friendly. FlexHousing features add convenience and practicality to the functions of a home.

ACCESSIBLE

The FlexHousing concept is user-friendly. Everywhere you look—the room dimensions, the location of controls, the detailing—you see smart, practical features. This common-sense approach is people-centred design that makes the many tasks of daily living easier and more pleasant.

People's lives are busy, and housekeeping can be a full-time job.

A FlexHouse is smart design suitable for everyone.

Safety begins with knowing where the dangers are and planning around them.

Easy-access light switch

flooring prevents falls in kitchens, bathrooms and laundry rooms. Handrails that start before the top of a flight of stairs and continue a short way past the bottom guide and support occupants.

Safety begins with knowing where the dangers are and planning around them. Such features add to the comfort and well-being that FlexHousing provides.

Accessibility and security

Many homeowners feel threatened by crime. Burglary, for instance, results in more than property loss—it robs people of the peace and privacy they expect in their homes. Security is a basic element of design and construction in FlexHousing—not an afterthought. Pre-wiring for the installation of an alarm or surveillance system makes it easy for homeowners to take the measures they need to feel secure, while strong, easy-to-use locks and latches are standard FlexHousing features.

Security is a basic element of design and construction in FlexHousing—not an afterthought. Pre-wiring for the installation of an alarm or surveillance system makes it easy for homeowners to take the measures they need to feel secure.

During construction, correct wiring makes security simple.

FlexHousing features add value to every home.

AFFORDABLE

Designing and building a home with FlexHousing features usually costs no more than building a conventional home. Although some features may be slightly more expensive than their standard counterparts, they recover their initial expense over the long term because pre-engineered features allow for easy and inexpensive change and renovation.

FlexHousing features recover their initial expense over the long term because pre-engineered features allow for easy and inexpensive change and renovation.

FlexHousing can incorporate durable, reliable and economical materials in well-planned designs. Builders and developers who take this approach spare homeowners the pain of unexpected maintenance and repairs later on. In addition, homes that incorporate FlexHousing principles offer a great deal more flexibility and comfort than conventionally built homes. This makes them desirable to consumers and a superior investment over the long term. The emphasis on convenient, practical features that enhance the comfort of the home and the ability to evolve into exactly what homeowners need can increase the resale value and marketability of this type of housing.

Ultimately, FlexHousing is the design of living spaces that do not become obsolete. This is done only through careful selection of building materials and good planning and design. In a FlexHouse, buyers purchase a home that provides the space they require today, with the option of adapting it later if their needs change. They enjoy its unique characteristics as long as they live in it, and if they ever decide to move, they reap the benefits of a high resale value—proof that their investment was wise.

> **The emphasis on convenient, practical features and the ability to evolve into exactly what home-owners need can greatly increase the resale value and marketability of this type of housing.**

HEALTHY HOUSING

FlexHousing design can include Healthy Housing principles. Today, homebuilders can build using healthy building materials and innovative housing technology that actually protect the health of the occupants and the environment. These homes can be designed to sit on less land, or to include mechanical systems that improve the quality of the indoor air. Energy efficiency, another Healthy Housing principle, can also be part of the FlexHousing approach. With the improved efficiency of today's heating, ventilation and air conditioning systems, consumers save on utility costs, use fewer natural resources and have more control over their home's environment than ever before.

Energy savings and quality construction pay off.

RESALE

If the day comes that you ever have to sell your house, you'll be proud to show off its smart design and people-friendly features. Potential buyers who tour a FlexHouse will see and appreciate its unique features.

From the wide, well-lit front entrance offering unhindered access to the home's interior to its extra-wide halls and easy-to-find light switches, the smart design is evident at every turn.

FlexHousing offers buyers freedom of choice. They can create the home they want, with the features they want, at different stages of their lives. FlexHousing offers the invaluable advantage of long-term cost-effectiveness, bringing real savings in utility and maintenance costs while providing a capital investment that is sure to yield substantial rewards.

Never having to say, "We're

Nicholas Varias

Nicholas Varias, an architect from London, Ontario, designed the FlexHouse that won Canada Mortgage and Housing Corporation's 1996 FlexHousing Design Competition. The challenge was to design a multi-purpose home that, with very little effort, could change according to the family's needs. This house is on display at the Canadian Centre for Housing Technology at the National Research Council in Ottawa as an example of the best in housing innovation and technology.

Varias has been living since 1990 in a home that he designed and built with FlexHousing features. The lower floor is a self-contained unit, once occupied by his wife's day-care business and now a guest suite for visiting relatives. The unit could be rented out as an apartment.

The Canadian Centre for Housing Technology in Ottawa

His design addresses the need for neighborhood spirit and community.

"People don't know their neighbours, and the elderly and people with disabilities are sent to live in special places," he says. "In the FlexHouse, everyone has a place in the home, both young and old."

His award-winning design is illustrated by Amanda's story. It shows how a typical home built according to FlexHousing principles can easily be reconfigured to accommodate families in flux.

The National Research Council consults and plans to ensure best results.

moving"

Amanda's Dream House

Amanda Smart, a hard-working young teacher, had struggled long to afford her first house. Single and full of ideals, she wanted a place to call her own, a place where she could paint the walls without asking for permission, where she could plan and build as her budget allowed.

It was 1998 and Amanda visited many homes. But when she first stepped through the front door of a FlexHouse, she knew this was a house for a lifetime. Like other new homes, it was beautiful, but something was different. This home was clearly designed to allow for future adaptations to match the changes life would bring and her ability to pay for new features. It was also brighter than the other homes she had seen, and the details seemed friendly and comfortable. Amanda knew she could be happy here.

Amanda bought the three-storey, semi-detached home, even though her mother asked, "Why do you need such a big place? You're young. You should buy a starter home and move up later." Amanda shrugged. She knew something her mother didn't.

In the course of time, Amanda rented the ground floor to Darren Strong, a law student at the nearby university. With the extra income, she was able to pay the mortgage and even put money away for retirement.

FlexHouses can be single homes, semi-detached, even row houses or high-rise apartments. Amanda bought the right-hand side of this semi-detached house.

Key features include adjacent direct access to the outside at ground level, wider doorways, lever handles on all doors, and good circulation space in hallways and rooms.

Darren's apartment is on the ground level. The rental income it provides enables Amanda to pay her mortgage. Her unit has both an inside and outside entry and an unfinished attic.

The house is built on a slope, so there's a walk-out basement at the back of the house, adding additional good-quality living space.

The staircases in the house can either be open to all levels or enclosed to separate self-contained units.

Life was comfortable and Amanda grew to love her neighbourhood with its interesting shops and friendly people. Then something happened quite unexpectedly. Amanda and Darren became friends. They shared the laundry facilities and the garden. They planted vegetables and flowers in the backyard. They loved astronomy and watched the stars—she on the balcony, he on the patio. One night, as they watched together from the garden, they fell in love.

In 1999, Amanda and Darren married and lived upstairs. He finished his studies and converted the downstairs bedroom into a home office and small bedroom. Because it was a FlexHouse, the unit was pre-designed to make this a relatively easy and economical conversion. A partition was easy to install, and each room had its own window, closet, wiring and lighting. The floor finish allowed the partition to be easily inserted.

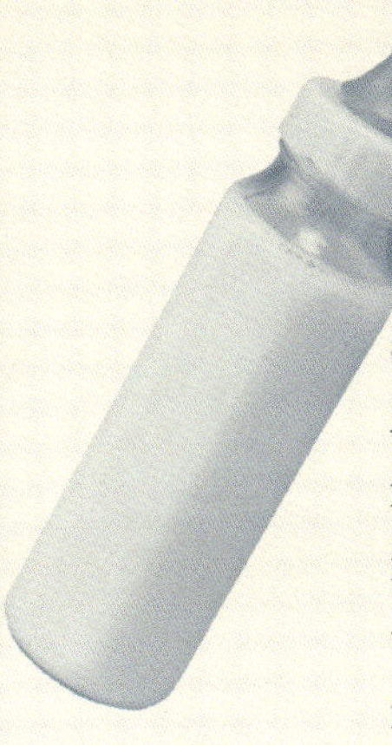

A year later, baby Alexander came along. Responding to their immediate needs, Amanda and Darren adapted the ground-floor washroom to serve also as a laundry room. All the required plumbing fixtures were in place for the change—they had been installed (much more cheaply) when the FlexHouse was built.

Soon afterwards, Amanda's mother, forgetting any doubts she ever had about the FlexHouse, moved in to help look after the baby. Amanda's sports car was traded for a minivan.

The four—grandmother, mother, father and son—had a rich family life, each in their own private space, which the FlexHouse provided with good soundproofing and separate entrances. Alexander grew healthy and strong. He dug up the vegetables that Mom and Dad planted and learned from Grandma about the same stars that had enchanted his parents.

Because Alexander's parents needed extra room, they renovated the attic to include a new master bedroom with an ensuite bathroom and walk-in closet. This was their "little paradise." Best of all, the conversion was relatively inexpensive.

The attic space had been pre-wired for lighting, electricity, cable and telephone. Even the staircase had reinforcement added to its wall during the initial construction should the need for an elevator ever arise.

Bliss, however, cannot last forever. Six years later, in 2006, Grandma's arthritis worsened, and she needed a wheelchair, so Amanda and Darren decided to adapt the house to make it easier for her to get around. Using the stacked closet space pre-designed for an elevator, they installed a lift to allow Grandma free access to all floors. The ground-floor laundry area was converted into a wheel-in shower. Grandma continued to play an active role in the family, and life went on as usual.

Several years later, Grandma died. By this time,

Other changes at this time included the addition of grab-bars in the toilet and shower area, and the removal of the vanity beneath the sink to allow clear space for a wheelchair.

Features already in place include easy-to-use lever faucets for adults and children. A mirror mounted flush with the level of the backsplash can be easily used by a person in a wheelchair or a child.

Darren had moved his office downtown. Alexander, now a teenager, was happy to move downstairs into the apartment, and his parents were very happy about the good sound separation between the two parts of the home. This had been pre-engineered by applying a skim coat of concrete. For two glorious years, Alexander enjoyed the freedom of a bachelor before he left home for university.

Once again, Amanda and Darren found themselves alone. Since the house was now too big for them, they decided to rent out the ground-floor apartment and use the money to help pay Alexander's tuition.

When Alexander returned home from college, it was with Rachel, his young bride. Like many newlyweds, they were penniless and needed a place to live. Amanda and Darren decided to help out by offering them the ground-floor apartment. Alexander and Rachel moved in. The apartment and basement below provided a perfect starter home for the new couple. They had all the freedom they desired at a price that enabled them to have a comfortable lifestyle while paying off their student loans.

Three years later a beautiful grandchild was born. Alexander, Rachel and the baby

needed more space, so they moved to the second-floor apartment. The "little paradise" on the third floor was large enough for

The two rooms near the entrance have any number of uses: bedrooms, home office, playroom or hobby room. The layout of this area makes it easy to convert them back and forth.

The key to these successful changes is the location of the windows, doors, light switches and outlets. A divided closet and suspended T-bar ceiling make such room transformations easy.

Amanda and Darren. Thus the two families switched living spaces within the same house, each benefiting from living space that suited their needs. Amanda also rented out the ground floor again to add to their retirement nest egg.

When Amanda and Darren retired, they wanted to be closer to their beloved garden, so they moved into the ground-floor apartment. The growing young family found a renewed pleasure in moving upstairs. Rachel and Alexander established themselves in their professions, and the rent they paid for the upstairs suite helped Amanda and Darren enjoy a comfortable retirement lifestyle.

The growing family benefits from the increased space of the second-floor unit, seen here from the living room. The attached greenhouse was an option added to the original house. The south-facing aspect of the main living spaces takes advantage of the sun's solar energy. The building was designed with energy-efficient construction details and windows.

Amanda's FlexHouse had indeed been a house of promise. From starter home to retirement dream, it had fulfilled the housing needs of her and her family for four decades.

The Moral of the Story

From its simple beginning as a basic starter home for a young person, this FlexHouse was able to grow and adapt to the changing needs of Amanda and her family. In the same way, FlexHouse designs also adapt to the various needs of different owners over time. Key to the success of this home was its affordability as an entry-level home and through all its adaptations and conversions over the years. Most important, this accessible home provided convenience and financial security as both a single-family home and an income property.

FlexHousing

CHOICES

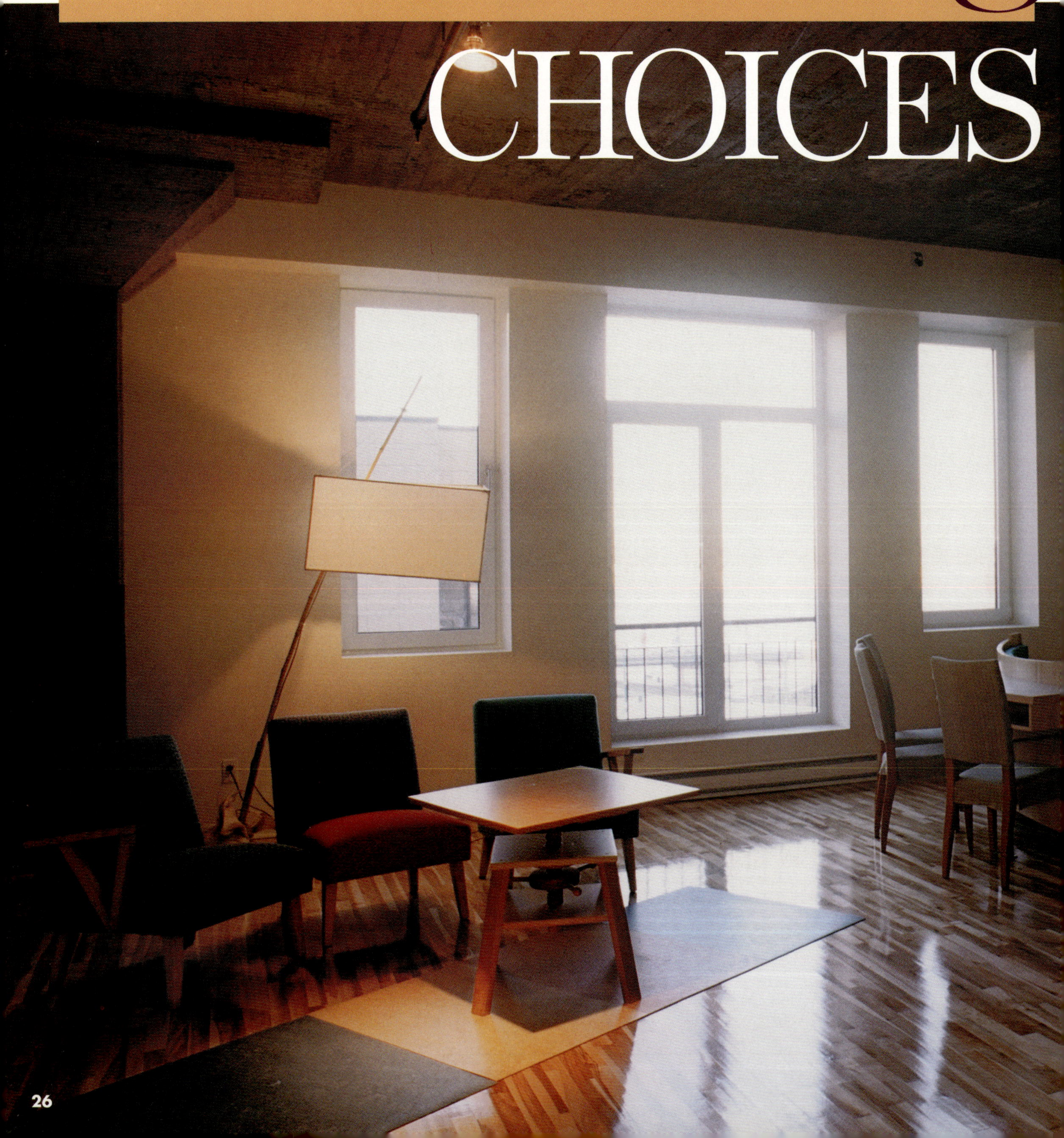

In neighbourhoods across Canada, more and more builders are creating houses, apartments and condominiums that include FlexHousing features. From the urban chic of Montréal to high-rise living in Edmonton, developers are designing and building dwellings to provide occupants with adaptable, flexible space and user-friendly features they'll appreciate for a lifetime.

Many of the homes pictured here are featured in a CMHC report by architect Pierre Teasdale.

What puts the flexibility in FlexHousing is its design principles. They can be applied to any type of housing—new houses, old houses, singles, duplexes, triplexes, apartments and condominiums.

Homes built to FlexHousing design principles come in a variety of shapes and layouts. They fit into any neighbourhood. For example, in downtown Montréal, where the streets are lined with duplexes and triplexes, a FlexHouse can be a single-family infill home that blends in with the surrounding homes and preserves the architectural character of the neighbourhood.

No matter where you find FlexHousing, whether it's in the downtown core or suburbia, FlexHousing demonstrates the adaptability, accessibility, affordability and convertible space that people will demand in the 21st century.

The examples of FlexHousing from cities across Canada show that FlexHousing is not one single design but an approach to adaptable, accessible, affordable and convertible living space.

Petite Maison Delanaudière, MONTRÉAL, QUÉBEC

This townhouse close to the heart of Montréal was **designed to be completed in stages by its owner.** It has lived up to its promise of adaptability and affordability. **Delivered as a rough-finished house to keep the purchase price down and allow the owners to work on it themselves,** it turned their labour into equity in the home. The birth of their first child was the incentive needed for the owners to finish the house themselves. During the first phase (May to September 1991), they finished the ground floor; during the second phase (1993–95), they finished the second-floor mezzanine and the terrace; in the third phase (1998), they finished the basement. The garage served as a workshop, where the couple could assemble components of the house without disrupting their living space. On the other hand, their neighbour, a single man, who lives in a similar unit next door, hasn't changed his house much from the original.

The home is also extendable. The owners can add a greenhouse on top of the porch above the garage or on top of the third-floor terrace. The basement is designed to be easily transformed into a studio apartment without major structural changes.

The Sprout House,
MONTRÉAL, QUÉBEC

The Sprout House in Montréal is **an excellent example of flexible design and affordable price.** The house started as a small, four-level building, 6 m (20 ft.) wide and 7 m (23 ft.) long. Growth potential is built into the house. The basement and attic are designed to be finished cost-effectively later. As part of the initial design, the basement has separate access, making it easy for the owners to create a separate unit. And the attic can easily be transformed into a family space, playroom, office or big master bedroom.

An addition at the back of the house makes it possible for the owner's mother to live close to the family while keeping her privacy—an arrangement that encourages social interaction and, of course, babysitting. **Basic plumbing has been in place from the start, making it easy to install a bathroom or kitchen addition later.** The owners can alter and renovate with little disruption to the basic existing structure, which reduces the cost of modifications. The owners can do most of the work themselves—a great way for young homeowners to convert their labour into capital in the form of home equity. The result is a starter home that is affordable for many potential buyers.

The Sprout House starts small but can grow in a number of ways.

Maison de Ville Adaptable, MONTRÉAL, QUÉBEC

This three-storey townhouse on St. Denis Street in Montréal is an example of **elegant infill housing between existing duplexes and triplexes.** The floors and walls are actually panels of steel beams and concrete, giving the house superb sound absorption and fire resistance. In the heart of Montréal, this is an ideal home for a young family, childless couple or singles because the space can be used in many different ways. The ground floor and the second-floor mezzanine are multi-purpose. On the mezzanine level, sliding doors disappear into the wall, making it possible either to open up the space or divide it. Shown below are two potential uses for the second floor. The first photograph shows the second floor used as child's bedroom. The second photograph shows it as an office with an attached reading room in the mezzanine area.

The photograph above shows the second floor used as child's bedroom. The photograph at right shows it as an office with an attached reading room in the mezzanine area.

Quai de la Commune, MONTRÉAL, QUÉBEC

This converted warehouse is ideal for the FlexHousing lifestyle.

Quai de la Commune is an 80-unit apartment building that began life as an industrial building in Old Montréal. The apartment units are hybrid lofts—a mix of unfinished lofts and finished apartments that feature high ceilings (3.7 m [12 ft.] on the ground floor and 3.3 m [11 ft.] on other floors). The open-concept living spaces vary in size from 76 to 113 m^2 (818 to 1,216 sq. ft.).

These units are easy to expand or contract. **People who need more space can either combine two back-to-back units or link two vertically aligned units with a staircase.** Every floor has complete electrical and mechanical fittings. **People in large apartments who need less space can subdivide their units into two smaller apartments without having to re-engincer thc electrical and mechanical services.** The open concept gives free rein to the occupants' creativity. Raised floors and lowered ceilings mark different-use areas such as bedrooms.

The space occupied by these stairs could accommodate an elevator if necessary.

Building floor plan

Riverwind Towers, EDMONTON, ALBERTA

Close to downtown Edmonton, two futuristic towers of **20 floors each illustrate FlexHousing design in a high-rise.** Each tower contains 57 apartment units, three on each floor. Unlike in traditional high-rises, each floor has one "mingle" unit in which people who may or may not be related live comfortably in the same apartment, sharing a common living space.

The mingle unit bedrooms are on each side of a central area containing a common living room, dining room and kitchen. The layout ensures maximum privacy for the two bedrooms, each of which has its own bathroom and balcony. Six separate thermostats control heating and cooling in different areas throughout the space. **The innovative mingle units are ideal for a couple with different work shifts, a couple with young adult children, an elderly person and a nurse, two unrelated people, or a couple that needs a home office.**

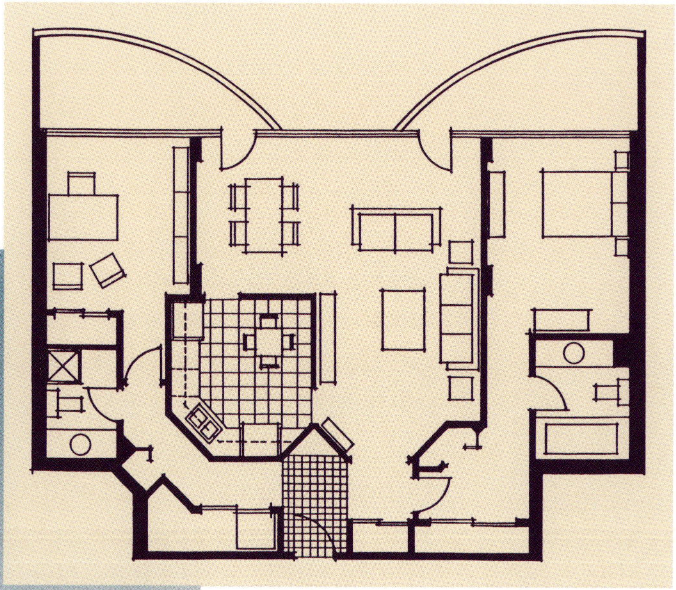

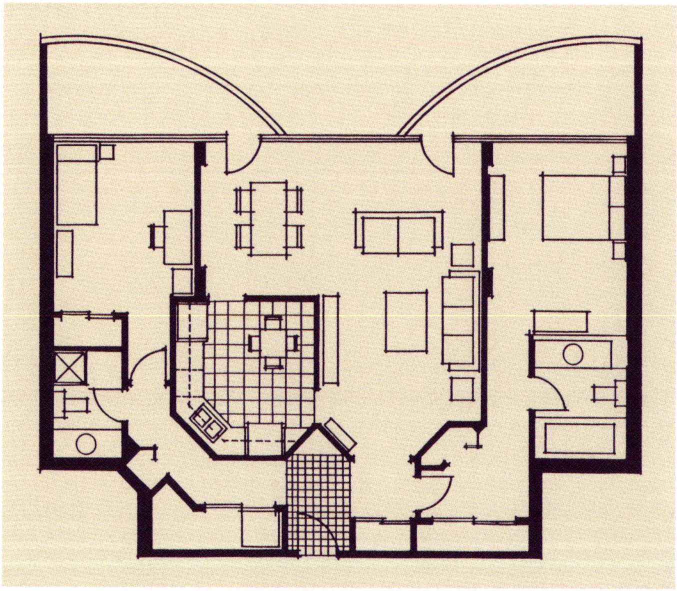

FlexHousing designs accommodate modern lifestyles.

Collette Nap
OF ST. JOHN'S, NEWFOUNDLAND

Collette Nap of St. John's has designed **single-storey homes that offer exceptional value and options usually found only in expensive custom-built homes.** The interior space allows ease of movement and is adaptable to the changing needs of single adults, young couples, families with a single child, and active seniors. The verandahs create the ambience of a traditional community while giving the occupants privacy.

Heart of the City,
EDMONTON, ALBERTA

The home that grows (Design 1), by Ron Wickman Architects and built with Habitat for Humanity, is **a basic single-family house that can expand over time through the progressive addition of living spaces at the back.** As these are added, they begin to enclose and embrace the outdoor spaces by creating a U-shaped courtyard.

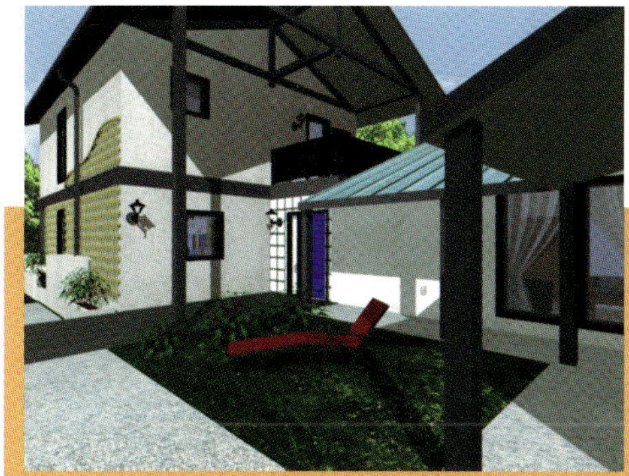

Design 1 **Planned expansion maintains outdoor living space.**

Modern FlexHouse in Newfoundland

Design 2

This infill triplex in Edmonton nurtures community spirit.

This triplex (Design 2) by Ron Wickman Architects includes many FlexHousing features in its U-shaped design. The plan provides **flexible living space for three families** and features stacked closets, straight-run stairs and rooms with potential for a home-based business near the entrances. The courtyard encloses a warm, protected space for young families or older residents.

The Design Workshop, PLAINFIELD, ONTARIO

The Design Workshop of Plainfield offers this FlexHousing solution to changing family needs. **This house can be finished in stages as family finances dictate.**

Radiant Homes and S.H.E. Consultants, ARMDALE, NOVA SCOTIA

Radiant Homes and S.H.E. Consultants of Armdale have designed **a two-bedroom starter home with built-in expandability. As the family grows, the owners can easily expand the living space into the attic.** The upper floor can also be made into a separate suite with a private entrance. The southern face of the house boasts a gorgeous two-storey window that floods the living area with light—an exceptional design for a young family starting out.

This beautiful, affordable FlexHousing design offers an opportunity for passive solar heating.

Norgate House Design Group, VANCOUVER, BRITISH COLUMBIA

The Norgate House Design Group has built adaptability, accessibility and affordability into Norgate House, a multi-level apartment complex in a beautiful North Vancouver location. **Designed for active seniors, Norgate House offers accessibility and many design possibilities for its owners.** Most units have a movable wall partition that

This design provides a variety of outdoor spaces as well as a bedroom with easy access to the bathroom and living areas.

slides between the bedroom and living area on a heavy-duty track. This unique feature turns a typical apartment layout into a flexible, airy space with the feel of a loft. Special attention has also been given to accommodation for caregivers and to fixtures that provide convenience and ease of use for people with varying degrees of ability and disability.

User Friendly Homes,

VANCOUVER, BRITISH COLUMBIA

This home of the future by User Friendly Homes of Vancouver demonstrates features that many people will want. Built in Maple Ridge, British Columbia, it is a 242 m^2 (2,600 sq. ft.), basement-entry unit **designed to meet the needs of an aging population.** It features spacious halls and entranceways and small details such as wall plugs positioned 460 mm (18 in.) above the floor rather than the usual 300 mm (12 in.), lower light switches and heat controls; and maximum standard-width doors with no raised sills to trip over. Kitchen features include multi-height counters and a dishwasher elevated for stacking ease.

Ensuite bathroom

A flush threshold (left) leads to a beautiful interior.

Stacked closets converted for an elevator

Straight-run stairs

This design eliminates the threshold, keeps the main floor at porch level and protects the entry against the elements.

Guildcrest's Tiger Lily, CLIFFORD, ONTARIO

In Clifford, Guildcrest Homes offers the Tiger Lily. This example of FlexHousing is **the perfect starter home—an innovative design that allows the home to grow as the family grows.** The Tiger Lily starts out as an affordable 93 m^2 (999 sq. ft.), two-bedroom bungalow. When the family needs additional space, and as means allow, the second storey can be finished to provide up to 152 m^2 (1,634 sq. ft.) of living space with three bedrooms, a main-floor family room, an eat-in kitchen and two full baths. It also has potential home-office space near the main entrance. Passers-by see a traditional Victorian exterior, but inside, this house looks to the future.

Phase 1

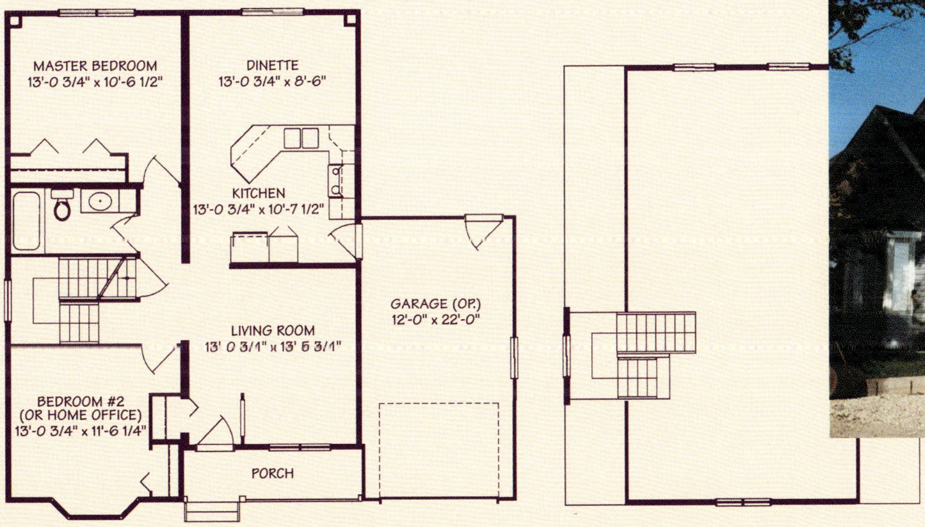

Multi-use space and room to grow

Phase 2

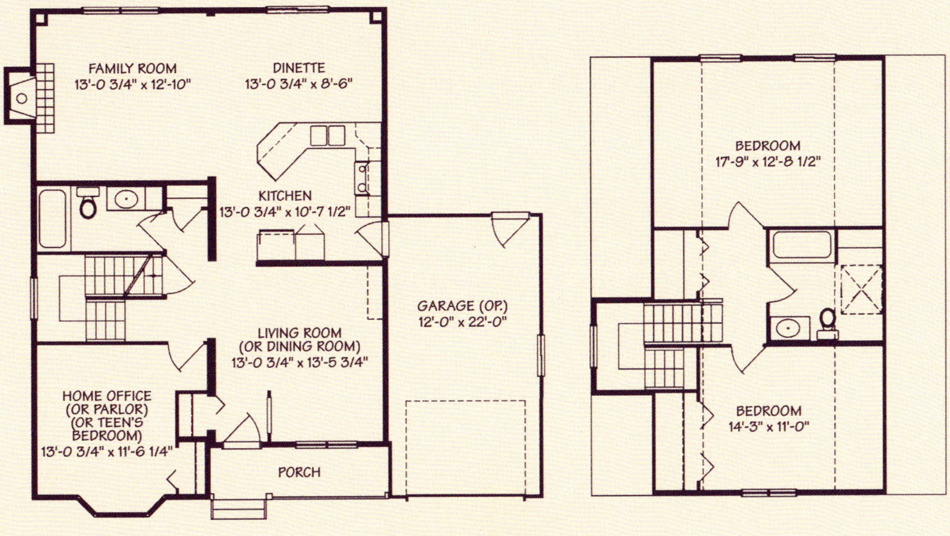

Practical features for BETTER LIVING *every day*

Turning FlexHousing design principles into actual features is a three-stage process. First, the new building or renovation must be designed to permit maximum flexibility. This requires careful forethought. Second, the ideas must be put down on paper. Third, steps must be taken to ensure that the contractor understands and produces the concept.

If a room is intended for use as a home office or large bedroom, with the possibility of adding a dividing wall to create two smaller bedrooms, there are several factors to consider. A home office is likely to need several well-located electrical outlets and telephone jacks. A bedroom needs closet space. And both will benefit from at least one window.

When the space is divided into two smaller rooms, each room will need light switches, electrical outlets, closet space and perhaps phone jacks. That means the original one-room design must distribute all of these elements so that when the space is partitioned, everything is available in both new rooms.

When the logistics of design have been worked out, the individual elements must be chosen. There are many options, from non-slip flooring and lever door handles to adjustable-height shelving and low-gloss, low-emission, washable finishes. Each contributes to the safety, accessibility, adaptability and healthiness of the home. They are also practical features for better living every day.

Taking a tour

To appreciate how FlexHousing features improve the design and function of a typical home, it's best to make a room-by-room study. The following sections look at the standard elements of most homes and determine how, with a little forethought, they can be made to open up a world of "flexible possibilities."

Parking spaces should be 2,800 mm (9 ft.) wide.

Paths should be between 1,100 mm (43 in.) and 1,500 mm (60 in.) wide with a slope of 1 in 20—100 mm in 2,000 mm (1 ft. in 20 ft.).

Entrances should have a clear, level space 1,500 mm (60 in.) by 1,500 mm (60 in.) on either side of the door.

The door should be between 865 mm (34 in.) and 910 mm (36 in.) wide with a threshold no higher than 19 mm (¾ in.).

Parking and Entrances

FlexHousing begins at the driveway. Parking spaces should be wide and connected to a firm, hazard-free path leading to the entrance of the house. There should be a covered space outside the door for shelter, and non-slip flooring on the inside for safety in wet winter months.

Entrances should be designed with security in mind. Adequate lighting and strong, easy-to-operate lever locks and latches are chief considerations. An adaptable design might be pre-wired for an intercom or closed-circuit TV monitor to help improve entranceway security

Parking spaces should be **wide** and connected to a **firm, hazard-free path** that leads to an entrance with a threshold **no higher than 19 mm (¾ in.).**

The Bathroom

A flexible bathroom accommodates a wide range of users. Free space on at least one side of the toilet improves accessibility, and space along the full length of the tub allows the taps to be reached from outside the tub without difficulty. This is convenient for parents bathing small children and makes cleaning the tub easier. A vertically adjustable hand-held shower can be mounted at different heights or used by hand for maximum flexibility. Areas that are often wet should have non-slip flooring, and a slip-resistant bathtub bottom is essential. Healthy Housing features such as water-conserving bathroom fixtures make FlexHousing environmentally responsible as well.

An aerator shower head can reduce water use by more than 60 per cent.

A standard-height toilet is appropriate for everyone: low-volume models reduce water use by 80 per cent.

Dual-lever faucets are easy to operate; single-lever and ball-type faucets can be confusing.

Water temperature regulators prevent scalding and burns.

The bathroom door should open outward to avoid obstructing the limited space inside.

Structural reinforcement of walls for grab-bars is an important safety feature. At some time, someone in the house may need the additional support. Using 16 mm (½ in.) plywood to reinforce areas behind and beside the toilet and around the three walls of a bathtub or shower provides the needed strength and makes installing supports much easier later on.

Dual-lever faucets are **easy to operate;** single-lever and ball-type faucets can be confusing.

SAMPLE COSTS

Bathroom wall reinforcement
$40 for 50 x 250 mm (2 x 10 in.) or **$90** for 16 mm (½ in.) plywood
versus
$530 for demolition, blocking and reconstruction

Change from tub to shower
very little when prepared for in original construction
versus
$2,900 if not prepared for in original construction

The Kitchen

L- or U-shaped open-concept layouts make it easy to reach everything in the kitchen. They also provide continuous counter space between appliances. Installing an adjustable-height work surface and an adjustable-height sink is not difficult and vastly improves the kitchen's accessibility for everyone. Pull-out work boards, at different heights, provide a choice of work surfaces.

Kitchen storage can be made more accessible with adjustable cabinet and shelf heights, and by installing full-extension shelves and drawers. Cabinets set on brackets are easily adjusted.

L- or U-shaped open-concept layouts make it easy to reach everything in the kitchen.

SAMPLE COSTS

Roll-out cabinet for additional storage under counter

Approximately **$211**

Counters beside cooktops, ovens and microwaves should be heat resistant.

Rounded corners on counters improve safety.

Energy-efficient appliances can cut energy consumption by 15 to 50 per cent.

Double sinks with overflow grooves and lever handles are easiest to use.

D-shaped handles on cupboards and drawers are sturdy and easy to grip.

D-shaped handles on **cupboards and drawers** are sturdy and easy to grip.

Rounded corners on **counters** improve safety.

THE Living Room

For flexible furniture arrangement, living rooms should have several electrical, telephone and cable outlets. If space is limited, living and dining rooms can be combined. Wiring for a ceiling fixture should be included in the design, allowing a fixture to be easily added later. Switches should be easy to reach from a sitting position, and there should be one outside the living room at the entrance, so people don't have to walk into an unlit area.

A doorless entry with no threshold creates an open feel and easy access.
A uniform level throughout is ideal, as abrupt changes interfere with accessibility and can be hazardous.

A **uniform level throughout** is ideal, as **abrupt changes** interfere with **accessibility and can be hazardous.**

THE Bedroom

Like the living room, the bedroom should permit a flexible furniture arrangement, adequate floor space around furniture, and storage. There should be at least enough room for a double bed. Providing for a bedroom and full bathroom on the ground floor can meet the needs of people with impaired mobility. Rooms designed to be expanded or contracted should be built so that walls can be removed or added without disruption to the floors, ceiling, windows or wiring.

Light switches should be at the **bedroom entrance** and close enough to the bed to be **switched on and off from the bed.**

There should be a free space of 1,500 mm (5 ft.) by 1,500 mm (5 ft.) on at least one side of the bed.

There should be clearances of 750 mm (30 in.) to 910 mm (36 in.) around other bedroom furniture.

Phone jacks and electrical outlets should be installed in several locations in the bedroom.

Light switches should be at the bedroom entrance and close enough to the bed to be switched on and off from the bed.

There should be a **free space** of **1,500 mm (5 ft.)** by **1,500 mm (5 ft.)** on at least **one side of the bed.**

SAMPLE COSTS

Installing or modifying light switches

$50 each when done as part of original construction
versus
$200 each when done after original construction

Installing or modifying outlets

$50 each when done as part of original construction
versus
$175 each when done after original construction

THE Laundry Room

A laundry room should be functional and convenient to work in. Front-loading machines with front-mounted controls are easiest to use. A work surface at which people can sit and fold laundry is a much-appreciated feature. Putting a laundry room on the ground floor or the same floor as the master bedroom is practical.

A balanced, wall-mounted **ironing board** adjustable to between **600 mm (2 ft.) and 850 mm (2¾ ft.) high** can be moved out of the way easily when not being used.

Dryers stacked over washers should be at shoulder level with controls no higher than 1,200 mm (4 ft.).

A clear space of 750 mm (30 in.) by 1,200 mm (4 ft.) in front of machines makes loading and unloading easier.

There should be a washtub near the washer and dryer.

A balanced, wall-mounted ironing board adjustable to between 600 mm (2 ft.) and 850 mm (2¾ ft.) high can be moved out of the way easily when not being used.

Dryers stacked over **washers** should be at **shoulder level** with controls no higher than **1,200 mm (4 ft.).**

Hallways AND

Non-slip flooring is important in hallways, corridors and on stairs. Carpets, which provide a non-slip surface, must be well secured. If they aren't, they are a tripping hazard. Stairs are a frequent cause of household accidents, but proper design can make them safer for everyone. Handrails should run continuously along the full length of a staircase and around any intermediate landings. They provide support and let

Stairs should be **1,100 mm (43 in.) wide.**

Stairways

users know by touch where the stairs start and finish. Adequate lighting is also important for stair safety.

SAMPLE COSTS

Lever door handles
$8 more than standard door handles

Wider door (excluding frame)
$10 more than standard of 810 mm (32 in.)
versus
$1,000 each if changed after initial construction

Lift
$0 to stack closets
$230 to reinforce closets
$8,000 in a FlexHouse
versus
up to $20,000 in a conventional home

Hallways should be 1,200 mm (4 ft.) wide.

Stairs should be 1,100 mm (43 in.) wide.

Stairs should have a maximum tread depth of 280 mm (11 in.) from riser to riser and a maximum riser height of 180 mm (7 in.).

Stairs should be consistent and have a uniform number of steps with a minimum of three risers and a maximum of 12 risers per run.

Stair treads should be slip-resistant.

Nosings (the rounded, projecting edge of a stair tread) should not project. If they do, the maximum projection should be no more than 40 mm (1½ in.).

Closed risers should be used: feet can slip through open risers, causing people to fall.

Handrails should be 30 mm (1¼ in.) to 40 mm (1½ in.) in diameter, between 800 mm (31 in.) and 920 mm (36 in.) above stair nosings.

Handrails should extend 300 mm (1 ft.) plus the depth of a tread past the bottom riser and the top riser.

A better, more convenient home

Making the most of available space and thinking ahead about safety and changing needs are the major considerations in FlexHousing design. When applied to a house, the principles of FlexHousing transform a typical home into a place of extraordinary convenience and comfort that you and your family can enjoy for a lifetime.

Systems and

FlexHousing can incorporate the principles of Healthy Housing. Healthy Housing principles have a major effect on the comfort and well-being of occupants, and on the efficiency of house, apartment or condominium mechanical systems.

Indoor air quality, lighting and background noise have direct effects on occupant health. Careful planning and the wise use of healthy materials and efficient appliances can give occupants a great deal of control over their indoor environment.

Good designs reduce energy use by minimizing heat loss in winter and heat gain in summer. Efficient systems cut down on the consumption of electricity and other fuels; many use renewable energy sources. By starting with durable, environmentally friendly building materials and reducing construction waste, it is possible to use resources efficiently.

Today's building lots are often smaller than those of 20 or 25 years ago. FlexHousing makes more creative use of available space. Resource-efficient landscaping—for example, cisterns or rain barrels to capture rainwater for gardening—and alternative water and wastewater systems can be used.

Systems

Electrical systems and controls

It is important that electrical systems are flexible enough to meet the needs of homeowners, today and tomorrow. Flexibility can come from installing more electrical outlets than usual or installing ground-fault interrupter outlets and a breaker panel on the main floor. Childproof outlets are a valuable safety feature. Of the numerous types of electrical switches available, large rocker switches are the easiest to use.

Ideal height for light switches: between 840 mm (33 in.) and 1,050 mm (41 in.)

Ideal height for electrical outlets: 450 mm (18 in.)

Materials

Heating, ventilation and air conditioning (HVAC)

Today, homeowners have more control over their indoor environment than in the past. High-efficiency condensing furnaces, heat pumps and integrated space- and water-heating systems make precise, economical control of air and water temperature possible.

Compact Heat Recovery Ventilators (HRVs) recover 70 per cent of the heat from stale indoor air to improve indoor air quality and reduce heating costs. At the same time, an HRV continuously supplies fresh air to the home. Using low-emission polyvinyl chloride (PVC) gaskets in the duct system also improves indoor air quality. Filtration systems remove moulds, dust, pollen and other contaminants from indoor air. In the bathroom, ventilation is essential for controlling humidity and exhausting odours.

Careful design places ventilation intakes and exhausts in places where they won't allow air already expelled from the house to re-enter the house. For ventilation systems to operate efficiently, ductwork must be airtight and accessible for cleaning.

Advanced mechanical equipment provides control over the indoor environment.

Materials

© The Ottawa Citizen

Selection and installation of readily available materials improves the indoor air quality.

Walls and finishes

Using healthy building materials is one way to improve the indoor air quality of a FlexHouse. Spruce is an excellent wood for wall construction. Domestic, fast-growing and renewable, it has the lowest chemical content of all the softwoods, making it beneficial to the quality of indoor air.

Fibre-reinforced gypsum drywall creates very little dust and releases few volatile chemicals during installation. Low-density PVC foam tape and low-emission silicone caulking help form an airtight drywall barrier system that eliminates drafts, restricts the entry of pollutants and moisture, and reduces heat loss by 75 per cent.

Easy-to-clean wall finishes, such as low-gloss scrubbable finishes, ceramic tiles and washable sheet-wall coverings, should be used. Plaster walls are also easy to clean, as well as attractive and durable. Birch trim and moulding are excellent decorative choices when sealed with a low-odour finish, such as water-based dispersion urethane. Low-emission, water-based, semi-gloss paint is the best choice for kitchens and bathrooms.

Flooring

Flooring should be durable and easy to maintain. Ideally, flooring should be manufactured using the lowest amount of energy possible, and from renewable material. Rigid board insulation under the concrete slab in the basement enables the floor to hold 75 per cent more heat than without such insulation. Coating the surface of the concrete slab with a low-emission, water-based wax provides an easy-to-maintain finish that eliminates concrete dust.

In general, choose wood and tile flooring with some area rugs rather than carpeting. They are cleaner, safer and more adaptable because they are easier to fit and readjust when redecorating. In addition, homeowners prefer easy-maintenance flooring. Hardwood floors and no-wax vinyl tiles have permanent finishes and require very little care. Terrazzo and vinyl sheet flooring can be slippery when wet unless treated with slip-resistant coatings.

Unglazed, low-sheen ceramic tiles are excellent for slip resistance.

Carpeting should have a thick, tight weave of nylon, wool or cotton pile no higher than 7 mm ($\frac{1}{3}$ in.). Non-toxic, burn-proof carpets and carpet tiles are also recommended. Carpet tiles also have the advantage of being laid out in small, easily replaceable sections. To avoid slipping, carpets should be glued down with non-toxic adhesives. If underpads are used, they should be dense and of minimal thickness.

Low-emission, slip-resistant tile flooring adds safety and beauty.

A long-wearing, low-maintenance wood floor adds warmth and contributes to clean air.

FlexHousing and Aesthetics

The goal of FlexHousing design is to achieve practical results in beautiful ways, and that includes furniture and decorations. A home with FlexHousing features may present a slightly different starting point for a decorator, but like any other dwelling, it can be decorated in a variety of ways. From colonial style to minimalism, a FlexHouse can be furnished and decorated in a style that expresses the individuality and creativity of the occupant. In addition, many Canadian architects, designers and homeowners are forging an exciting new aesthetic through the marriage of the practical and the decorative that FlexHousing brings to life.

Adaptable and Spacious

Barbara Armstrong of Preston's Interiors decorated an ocean-view home designed by architect Steve Zibin in Surrey, British Columbia. Boasting many FlexHousing features, the home is highly functional, extremely accessible and filled with aesthetic pleasures. Zibin and Armstrong came up with solutions that satisfied the owners' functional needs while making the most of light, space, texture and colour.

Armstrong explains the challenge of decorating a home where accessibility is so strongly emphasized.

"Your approach to space has to change. When designers see an empty space, they tend to want to fill it. With barrier-free, you want to leave space open and make things accessible. I had to learn not to put something in those wide-open spaces."

In fact, the openness of this particular design becomes a key element of its appeal.

"When designers see an empty space, they tend to want to fill it. With barrier-free, you want to leave space open and make things accessible. I had to learn not to put something in those wide-open spaces."

The physical setting gives impressive views, and Zibin employed these views to the fullest. Large windows make it a veritable observatory for the changing seasons and bathe the interior space in natural light. Armstrong drew further attention to the outdoors by using neutral tones on the walls.

Choosing colours can depend—as in this case—on elements such as lighting and windows, or it can be a matter of taste. Armstrong loves colour and suggests "bright yellows or rich reds make for extraordinary rooms." In this home, she brings the visual equivalent of lemon zest to the rooms by placing colourful objects and works of art strategically throughout.

This house combines comfort and accessibility with great style.

Particular attention was given to the bathroom. The result is a charming version of a European spa, tiled from floor to ceiling. The luxurious walk-in shower is outfitted with benches and has room for two. Armstrong chose to work with small tiles because they can create an attractive and slip-resistant surface. Larger ceramic or granite tiles would require sandblasting to be made non-slip.

The Surrey home is a haven of good taste. Every room complements those adjoined to it. The combination of practical thinking and decorative savvy is finely made indeed.

An attractively tiled bathroom is safe and functional for everyone.

Expanding Horizons

Minto Developments Inc. of Ottawa and Toronto gained first-hand experience with the principles of FlexHousing in 1996 through the development of the home of the company's president, Roger Greenberg. The experience has influenced how the company designs housing projects and the options it now offers to all new homebuyers.

"Mr. Greenberg had special needs because his child uses a wheelchair for mobility," explains Bill Ritcey, senior architect for Minto. "The experience, however, opened our eyes to certain design features which were once considered only for people with mobility problems. For example, on-grade access is just a logical feature. Exterior stair entry to a home is just too awkward. For people with children, active seniors or just about anyone, comfortable access to the house is important."

"For people with children, active seniors or just about anyone, comfortable access into the house is important."

Accessibility and mobility in the design of the president's home show taste and creativity. In the family room, for example, a colourful geometric design has been inset into the hardwood floor. Like an area rug, it adds colour and definition to the space, but the kids won't trip on it. Upstairs, low-pile, wall-to-wall carpeting provides warmth, softens the sound of footsteps, traps far less dust than deeper carpets and gives a clean feel to the space.

Greenberg says that while this particular home is larger and has certain extras, the basic features that make it accessible are quite affordable.

"For an average home, lowering the height of the switches, raising the height of the wall plugs, making the plumbing fixtures accessible and using levered door handles instead of round doorknobs are not things that cost significantly more. Other features, such as wider entry doors and hallways, and wall reinforcements to accommodate future grab-bars, add minimally to the construction costs if planned intelligently in advance."

FlexHousing features are for every house, every taste and every budget.

"For an average home, lowering the height of the switches, raising the height of the wall plugs, making the plumbing fixtures accessible and using levered door handles instead of round doorknobs are not things that cost significantly more."

Dollars and Sense

Affordability is a fundamental principle of the FlexHousing concept. When people look at the itemized budget for a FlexHouse, it is slightly higher than the price of a conventional home of similar style and size. How does this translate into affordability?

The answer is in the short-term and long-term payback on the initial investment. The short-term payback comes from the energy efficiency that the addition of Healthy Housing features can provide. Low-emission windows, for example, typically cost 10 per cent more than other windows but are more energy-efficient. Savings on heating make up for that additional initial outlay in as little as three years. In areas of the country where household water use is charged by volume, the price of a rainwater cistern can be recovered in one summer. A Heat Recovery Ventilator (HRV) has many benefits for occupant health and recovers the initial cost over seven or eight years. These features also add to the value of the house.

More important, however, is the long-term recovery on investment. Because a FlexHouse is easily adaptable and less costly to renovate than a conventional home, it is useful to its occupants for a longer period of time.

This long-term recovery plan makes sense. The average homeowner in Canada renovates every three to five years at a cost of roughly $3,000. Every 10 years, 21 per cent of Canadians move once and an overwhelming 44 per cent move twice or more. **The two most common reasons for moving are to buy a first home and to buy a larger home.** When people move to a larger home, there are almost always costs of between $10,000 and $12,000 for legal fees, real estate and moving costs, not to mention one-time municipal taxes. A home that never outgrows its usefulness can reduce these expenses.

A FlexHouse is easy to renovate because it is designed to be renovated. FlexHouse owners can enlarge or reconfigure their houses to grow or change according to family needs. That saves money because there's no need to move when the family's needs change.

A FlexHouse is easily adaptable and therefore less costly to renovate than a conventional home.

Other savings are not as obvious or easy to calculate but just as worthy of consideration. There is always an emotional and social price to pay when moving into a new neighbourhood, and moving house puts a physical and mental strain on every member of the family.

When looking at the affordability of a FlexHouse, it is important to view it as a long-term investment that accommodates your changing lifestyle rather than a quick fix to your current housing needs. In addition to the monetary values, the choice of a FlexHouse includes a whole set of personal values, such as the importance of friendship, community and stability.

Cost scenario

1: A SOLUTION FOR REDUCING THE PURCHASE PRICE OF THE HOUSE

Peter and Christiane pay rent of $887 a month. To save money, they decide to buy a house. They are in their 30s and one day hope to have one or two children. They are looking for a house with about 120 m² (1,292 sq. ft.) of living space in a neighbourhood close to the centre of the city. Their combined gross annual income of $34,000 and savings of $5,000 would allow them to buy a property that would cost about $100,000. Unfortunately, the average cost of the homes that interest them in this neighbourhood is $125,000. After several weeks of intensive research, a sales agent suggests a new two-storey Sprout House of 80 m² (861 sq. ft.) with an unfinished basement and attic—each 20 m² (215 sq. ft.). The purchase price of $103,000 allows Peter and Christiane to become owners immediately and finish off the unfinished areas later. After making the calculations at right, Peter and Christiane don't hesitate to buy.

Situation before buying	
Monthly rent	$887
Situation after buying	
Monthly mortgage	$641
Monthly taxes	$172
Total	$813
Monthly savings	
Reduction in monthly payments	$74
Annual growth potential of 4% (by month)	$343
Amount contributed to equity per month	$141
Total	$558

Cost scenario

2: A SOLUTION TO REDUCE CHILD-CARE COSTS

Nicholas and Valerie have capital of $10,000. They live in a small, single-family home, which they own, in the suburbs. They are in their mid-30s and have an eight-month-old girl. They are both very busy with their respective jobs, and, on top of it, one or the other has to spend an hour every day transporting their daughter to a far-away day-care centre. Nicholas's mother, who is alone and available, would help look after the little girl in exchange for some services if she could find an apartment in the neighbourhood, but none exist. Nicholas and Valerie decide to expand the house to accommodate the grandmother by adding an accessory apartment of about 55 m^2 (592 sq. ft.) at a cost of about $45,000. The financial basis for their decision is given at right.

Annual situation before constructing the addition	
Day-care fees (240 days @ $20)	$4,800
Transportation to day-care centre (2,400 km @ $0.38 per km)	$912
Total	$5,712
Annual situation after building the apartment	
Loss of interest income on capital of $10,000	($700)
Mortgage payments	($2,760)
Heating costs	($400)
Municipal and school taxes	($900)
Annual income from the apartment	$4,500
Potential appreciation (4%) in the value of the apartment	$1,476
Amount contributed to equity	$627
Total	$1,843

Cost scenario

3: A SOLUTION TO REDUCE THE FREQUENCY OF MOVES

James and Suzanne are planning to retire. They own the duplex they have lived in for 17 years. At the time they bought it, the duplex was the only affordable housing with room for an office for each of them and room for five children from previous marriages. To change the duplex into a single-family home, they only had to take out a piece of the wall to create direct access from the main-floor living space. Recently, the last of the children left home, and James and Suzanne decided to change their home back into a duplex. The piece of the wall that had been removed was rebuilt and the upstairs apartment rented out.

The costs involved, perhaps for some plumbing and cabinets, were not significant. But the savings resulting from not having to sell their property and move to a more modest home were considerable. Their financial analysis is provided at right.

Real estate agent's commission for selling the duplex ($230,000 @ 6%)	$13,800
Legal fees resulting from the sale of the duplex	$200
Notary fees related to the purchase of a new home	$900
Architect's fees for evaluating a new home	$400
Moving costs	$1,000
Decorating costs for new house	$3,500
Total savings as a result of not moving house	$19,600

Cost scenario

4: A SOLUTION TO REDUCE THE COST OF OFFICE SPACE

Luke and Sylvia became a couple when they were in their 50s and were married about 10 years ago. At that time, Sylvia was the mother of one teenager from a previous marriage, and Luke had no children. They decided to rent a 90 m^2 (969 sq. ft.), two-bedroom, mingle-type apartment in a high-rise building. In this apartment, the bedrooms were located at the maximum distance from each other, and each had direct access to a corridor, a bathroom and a balcony. They chose this type of apartment thinking it would give everyone more privacy. They also anticipated that when the teenager left the house, Sylvia, who is a lawyer, would be able to move her office into the apartment. This two-bedroom, mingle-type apartment cost $10,704 annually, while a standard two-bedroom apartment of the same quality would cost $10,200 annually.

Recently, the teenager moved out of the house. Sylvia left the office she rented downtown and began working from her home. With its two entry points, the mingle apartment was perfectly suited to this use. It allowed Sylvia to receive clients in her home without disturbing her partner. Moving the office into the home also allowed her the extra savings shown at right.

Annual savings due to not renting office space downtown (15 m^2 [161 sq. ft.] @ $150 per m^2 [$14 per sq. ft.])	$2,250
Savings from not driving to the office (1,920 km @ $0.38 per km)	$730
Savings on parking at the downtown office (11 months @ $100)	$1,100
Additional annual cost of living in the mingle versus a standard apartment	($504)
Net annual savings	$3,576

Cost scenario

5: A SOLUTION TO REDUCE RENOVATION COSTS

Michael and Jean were looking for a single-family home. With the help of a real estate agent, they discovered two houses they liked, each with three bedrooms. Because they have only one child, their intention was to combine two of the bedrooms into one larger one with an ensuite bathroom. Before making a final choice, they asked an architect to tell them which of the two houses would be less costly to renovate. The floor of house A was built with T-joists, and there was no supporting wall as there was in House B, where the two rooms to be combined were separated by a supporting wall. The choice was not difficult to make because the architect told them that the cost of renovations would be no higher than $11,000 for House A and about $18,500 for House B. The $7,500 difference was the result of the extra work that would be required in House B.

Additional work required in House B

- The weight of the supporting wall would have to be transferred by adding a beam and columns.
- Concrete footings would have to be poured to support the columns.
- A large part of the floor and the ceiling would have to be demolished and repaired to bring the mechanical and electrical conduits together.

FlexHousing Winners

National Winner

The London FlexHouse

Nouvelle Development Corporation of London, Ontario, was the national winner of CMHC's 1996 FlexHousing Design Competition. The winning design can be built as a single-family detached, semi-detached or row house. Internal spaces are designed to be easily adapted after initial construction. Healthy Housing features make it healthy for the occupant and the environment. And it's barrier-free. The entrances, hallways, storage spaces, kitchen and washrooms are designed with safety and accessibility in mind.

Healthy, bright and brimming with Flex features

Features

- Exterior design and materials complement existing homes in the neighbourhood.
- Three-storey single unit can be subdivided into either two or three units.
- Rooftop terrace.
- Optional home office.
- Optional greenhouse on second or third floor.
- Large windows give occupants full outdoor views from a seated position.
- Wide hallways and stairwells reinforced for future stair-lift.
- Adjustable heights for kitchen and bathroom cabinets and counters.
- Scald-protective plumbing in kitchen and bathrooms.
- Laundry space can be adapted for a wheel-in shower.
- Ground floor is wheelchair-accessible, with optional stair-lifts and vertical lifts to all floors.
- Air temperature, humidity and air movement easily controlled.
- Materials with low-emission finishes.
- Good-quality, energy-efficient windows.
- Rainwater collection cisterns for outdoor gardening.

SAMPLE MAIN FLOOR PLAN

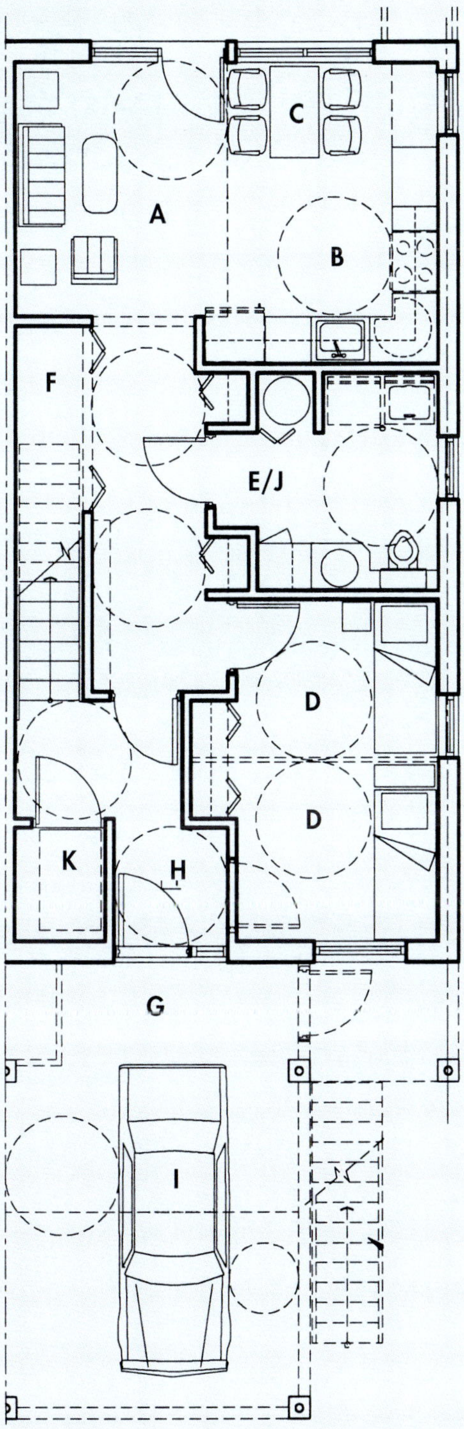

◌ Denotes manoeuvring space

ELEVATION

A – Living room	G – Deck/balcony
B – Kitchen	H – Vestibule
C – Dining room	I – Carport/garage
D – Bedroom	J – Utility garage
E – Washroom	K – Storage space/optional elevator shaft
F – Storage	

Multi-unit project prices

Two-storey units:
139 and 177 m² (1,500 and 1,900 sq. ft.)
Expected selling price: $125,000

Three-storey units:
177 and 279 m² (1,900 and 3,000 sq. ft.)
Expected selling price: $150,000

Award of Merit

The Montréal FlexHouse

This CMHC FlexHousing Award of Merit went to the Affordable Homes Program of the McGill School of Architecture and Anobid Construction Corporation of Montréal, Québec. Family comes first in this innovative design. The house can grow according to the occupants' needs. It can be purchased by the storey, both at and after initial construction. Each unit is wheelchair accessible and equipped with safety features. The designer has also employed an attractive contrast of colours and textures that aid orientation for people with vision difficulties.

Affordable, adaptable, smart and stylish

This stylish three-storey home has been built in an existing development in Le Boisé d'Auteuil.

Features

Floor plans are entirely adaptable to suit needs.

Large windows permit outdoor views from a seated position.

Buyers select the layout from a menu with components (kitchen, bathroom, etc.) and subcomponents (walls, grab-bars, toilets, etc.) and can modify or add to these selections as required in future.

Utilities, stairs and shell are the only permanent elements, allowing for easy modifications.

Stairwells are aligned and reinforced for easy installation of a stair-lift.

Ramps and balconies are optional.

Rooms are conceived for wheelchair mobility and ease of carrying out tasks.

Contrasting colours and textures of floors, walls and cabinetry aid in orientation.

Sinks and counters have knee space beneath.

Light switches, fixtures and counters are accessible from a seated or standing position.

SAMPLE FLOOR PLAN
MEZZANINE

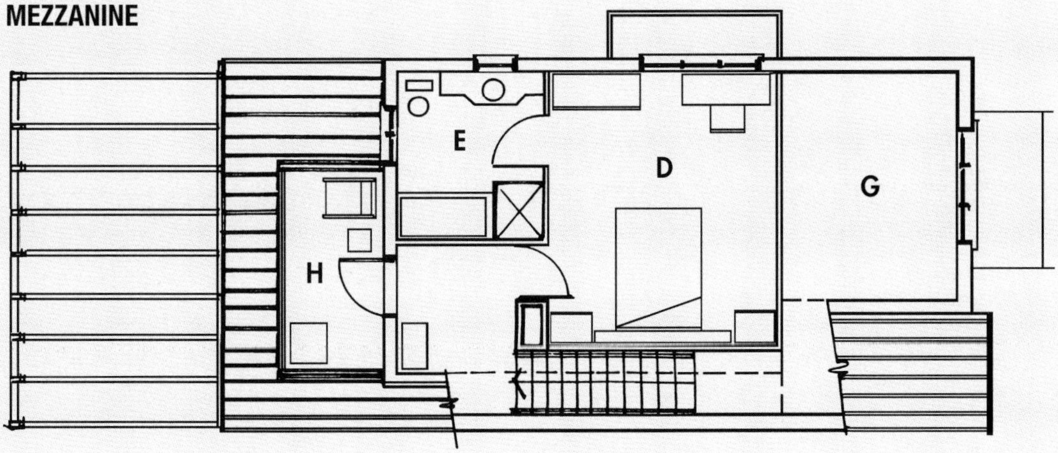

SAMPLE FLOOR PLAN
DUPLEX UNIT C—SECOND FLOOR

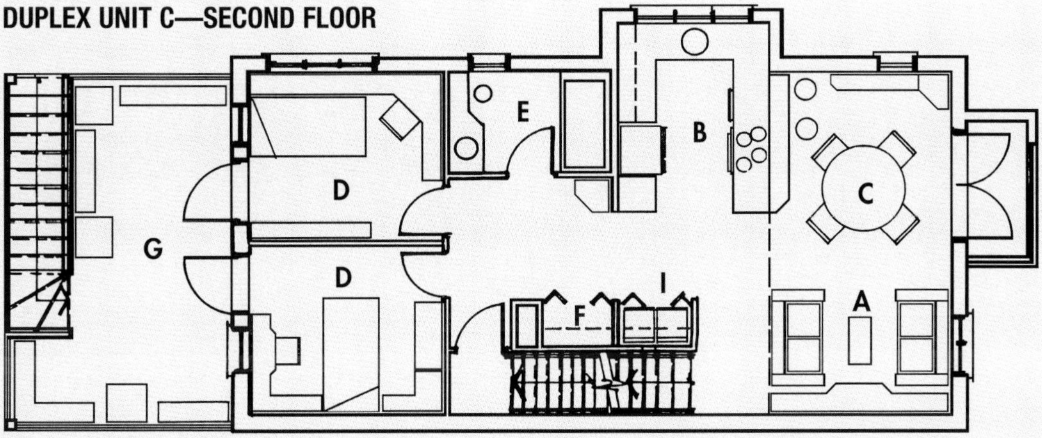

- A – Living room
- B – Kitchen
- C – Dining room
- D – Bedroom
- E – Washroom
- F – Storage
- G – Deck/balcony
- H – Den
- I – Utility room

SIDE ELEVATION

Prices

Single-family unit:
149 m² (1,600 sq. ft.)
(2 floors)
Selling price: $167,525

Duplex unit B:
74 m² (800 sq. ft.)
(ground floor)
Selling price: $79,441

Duplex unit C:
116 m² (1,250 sq. ft.)
(upper 1.5 floors)
Selling price: $81,916

Award of Merit

The Edmonton FlexHouse

This CMHC FlexHousing award-winning design was developed by the father and son team of Percy and Ron Wickman of Finalta Designs Inc. of Edmonton, Alberta. The Wickmans are leaders in housing innovation, aiming to create a house that addresses a multitude of issues including affordability, community interaction, accessibility, flexibility and home automation while using construction materials from sustainable resources. The Wickmans' design is a suitable starter home with two or three bedrooms that can be enlarged to encompass another suite and a home office. The front verandah and rear courtyard are especially suited for balancing the social and private lives of the occupants. The home is intended to grow with a family and, because of its creative use of a small lot, is well suited for inner city living. This project was built by the non-profit group Habitat for Humanity in Edmonton in 1997.

Simplicity and charm to grow with

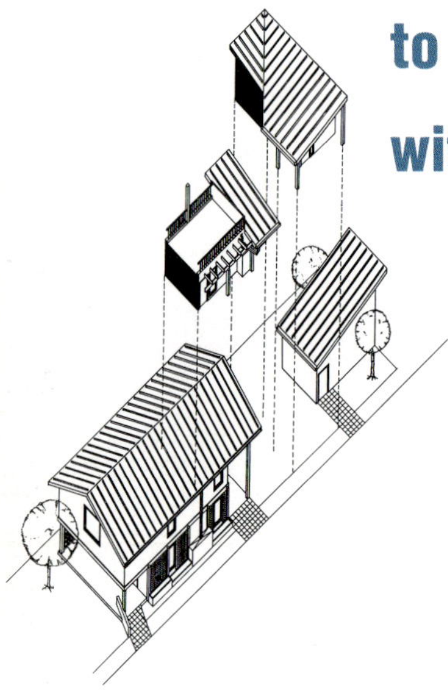

Features

- **Expandable design—from a 116 m^2 (1,250 sq. ft.) starter home to a four-bedroom, single-family home that includes a separate, self-contained suite.**
- **Front porch and courtyard to promote social interaction while maintaining a private garden space.**
- **Open floor plans.**
- **Grade access for people in wheelchairs.**
- **Adjustable kitchen counters, rod and shelf heights.**
- **Strategic use of colour, contrast and changes in texture of floor and wall surfaces as visual and tactile cues for people with sight and cognitive limitations.**
- **Structural reinforcements for future installation of a residential elevator, stair-lift and grab-bars.**
- **Lever door handles and accordion closet doors.**
- **Environmentally responsible materials with low gas emissions (off-gassing).**
- **Building materials made from recycled and waste materials.**
- **Rainwater cisterns for gardening.**

SAMPLE FLOOR PLAN—PHASE 1

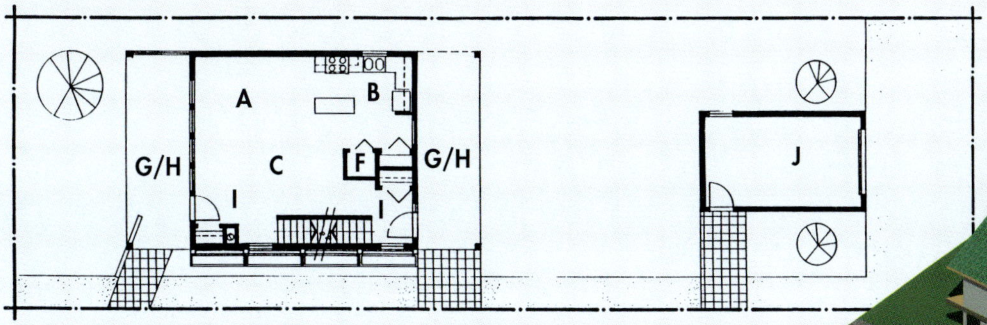

SAMPLE FLOOR PLAN—PHASE 2

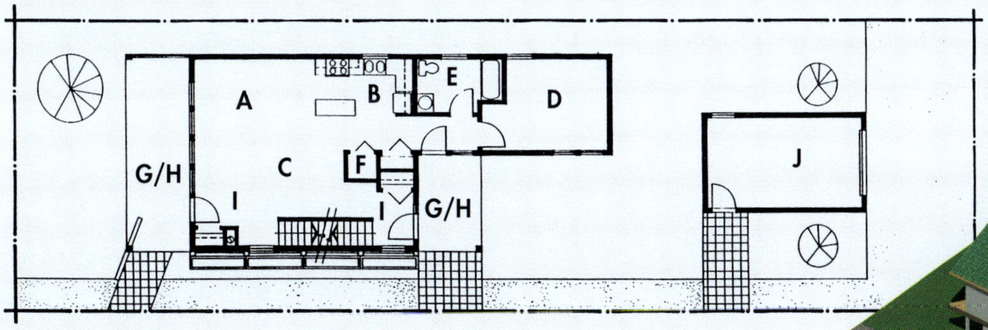

SAMPLE FLOOR PLAN—PHASE 3

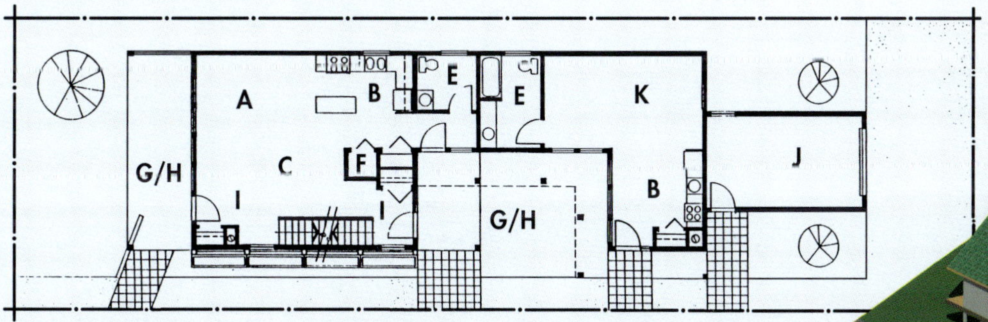

A – Living room	G – Deck/patio
B – Kitchen	H – Covered entry
C – Dining room	I – Vestibule
D – Bedroom on upper level	J – Garage
E – Washroom	K – Optional self-contained suite
F – Storage	

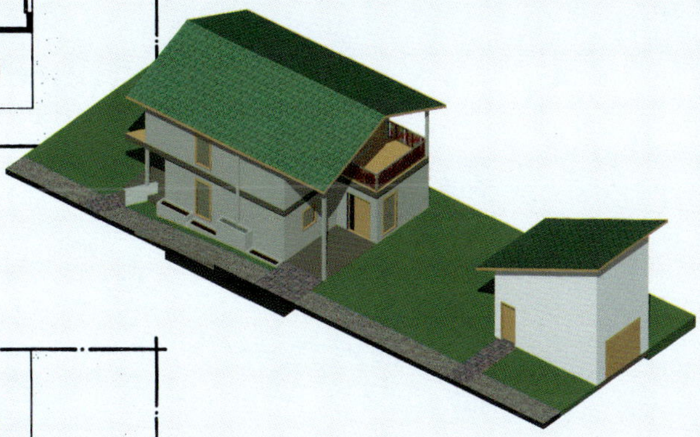

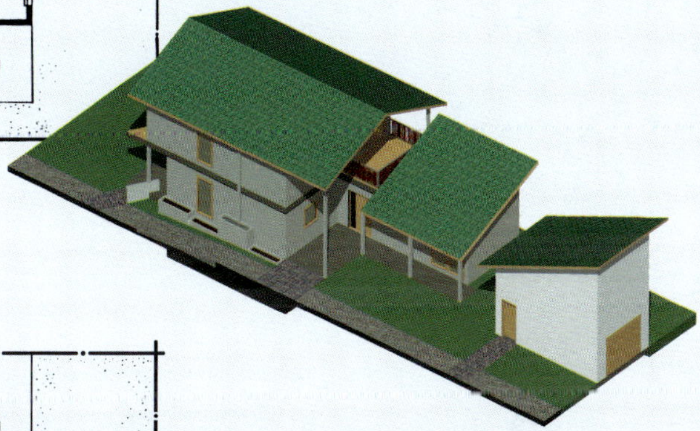

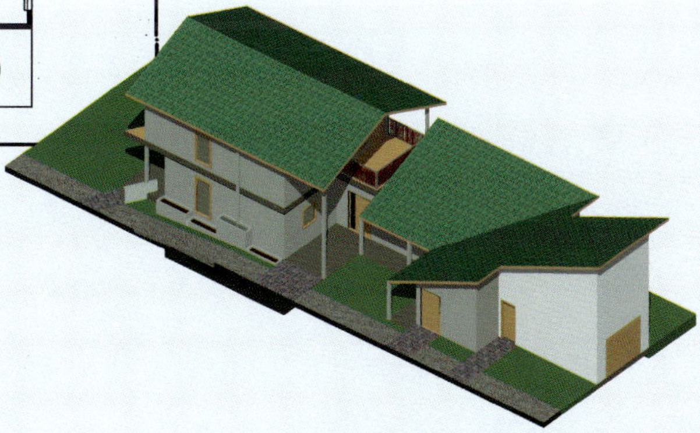

ELEVATIONS

Price

Starter dwelling:

116 m² (1,250 sq. ft.)
Selling price: $122,500

Award of Merit

The Saint-Jérôme FlexHouse

This CMHC FlexHousing award-winning design by Stéphane Hazan Architectes of Côte-Saint-Luc, Québec, is the ultimate in flexibility and elegance. Having the appearance of a carriage-trade home, this structure includes four large garden apartments with in-law or bachelor suites. It can also be broken up into smaller units for use as a nursing home or a student residence with seven to 10 units. Three of the four units are at ground level, providing easy access for wheelchairs. And each unit has a garage that can be converted into living space or a work area. This FlexHousing design is intended for a development in the town of Saint-Jérôme, Québec. Special attention has been paid to integrating a series of these structures into an existing neighbourhood and building on the north-south axis for maximum light.

Multi-purpose elegance

Features

- Private garden and connecting garage for each unit.
- All garages easily converted into bachelor apartments or work areas.
- Apartments and garages wired for home-office conversion.
- Apartments divisible into two or more units.
- Movable wall-frame panels allow greater flexibility as needs require.
- All necessary connections (plumbing, electricity, etc.) for the conversions in place and ready to use.
- Reinforced stairwells allow installation of a chair-lift.
- Adjustable heights for work surfaces and counters; duckbill door handles.
- Walls reinforced for grab-bars.

SAMPLE MAIN FLOOR PLAN

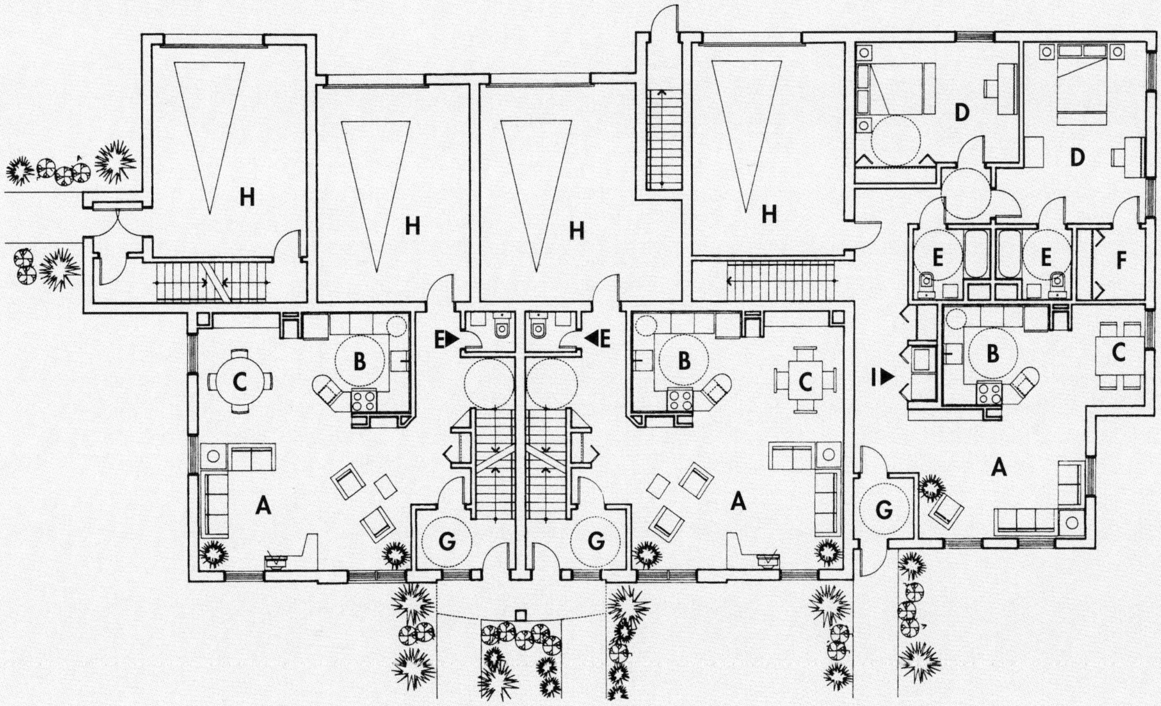

A – Living room
B – Kitchen
C – Dining room
D – Bedroom
E – Washroom
F – Storage
G – Vestibule
H – Garage
I – Utility room

◌ Denotes manoeuvring space

Prices

Bungalow:
149 m^2 (1,600 sq. ft.)
Selling price: $131,800

Cottage:
130 m^2 (1,400 sq. ft.)
Selling price: $122,900

Apartment:
102 m^2 (1,100 sq. ft.)
Selling price: $105,400

No basements are included in prices as site is bedrock.

FLEXCHEX

When you sit down with your architect or contractor, have your FlexHousing checklist ready to make sure you get the Flex features you want.

ESSENTIAL FLEXHOUSING DESIGN FEATURES

- On-grade access
- Covered entrances with level landings and adequate lighting
- Main living level containing kitchen, living room, washroom and a space suitable for bedroom or home office
- Design that permits double occupancy later
- Stairs should be straight-run and at least 1,000 mm (39 in.) wide
- Easily movable or removable partitions
- Good sound separation to ensure privacy

✓ On-grade access
✓ Covered entrances with level landings and adequate lighting

✓ Stairs should be straight-run and at least 1,000 mm (39 in.) wide

✓ Main living level containing kitchen, living room, washroom and a space suitable for bedroom or home office

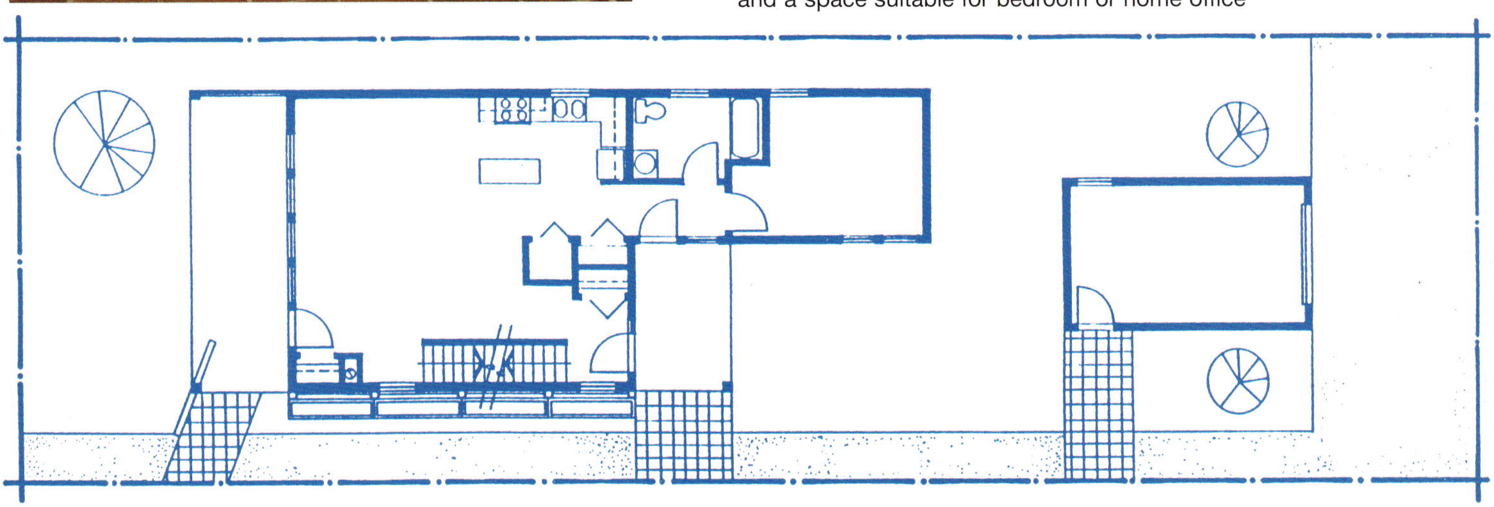

FLEXHOUSING CAN ALSO INCORPORATE ALL THE FOLLOWING FEATURES

SITE AND GENERAL CONSIDERATIONS

✓ Wide doors and hallways

- Gently sloped sidewalks and driveways
- Wide doors and hallways
- Bevelled thresholds, no higher than 19 mm (¾ in.)
- Most windows located on south-facing walls for maximum exposure to winter sun
- Low window sills
- Levered handles and easy-to-operate door locks
- Reinforced stairway walls to allow future installation of a stair-lift, or vertically aligned closets and appropriate framing to allow future installation of a vertical lift

✓ Low window sills

✓ Levered handles and easy-to-operate door locks

KITCHEN AND BATHROOM

- Non-slip flooring
- Clear floor space
- Task lighting over sink, stove and work surfaces
- Some electrical switches and outlets near front of counters

✓ Some electrical switches and outlets near front of counters

✓ Task lighting over sink, stove and work surfaces

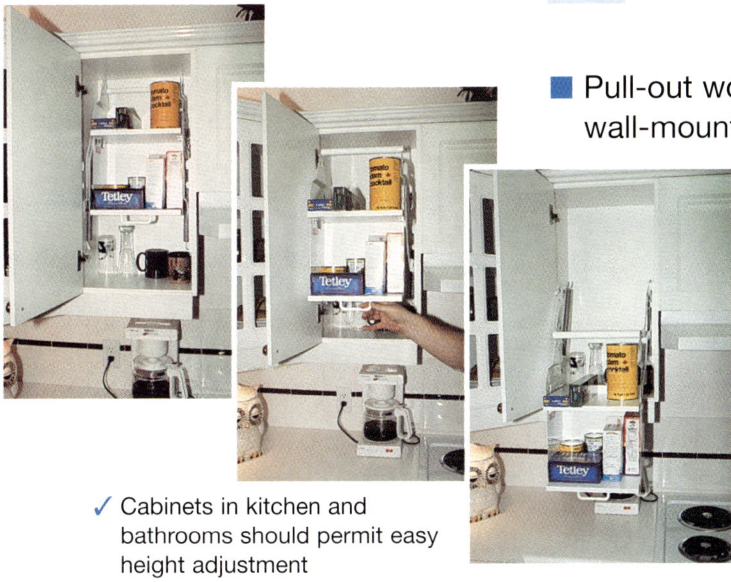

✓ Cabinets in kitchen and bathrooms should permit easy height adjustment

✓ Pull-out work boards; one close to wall-mounted oven

- Pull-out work boards; one close to wall-mounted oven
- Adjustable-height counters and sinks, or work surfaces at various heights
- Open space under sink and cooktop
- Wall reinforcement for grab-bars near bath and toilet
- Easy-to-use faucets, such as lever-type
- D-handles for drawers and cupboards
- Pressure-balanced temperature-regulating faucets
- Full extension drawers and shelves
- Cabinets in kitchen and bathrooms should permit easy height adjustment

✓ Wall reinforcement for grab-bars near bath and toilet

✓ Easy-to-use faucets, such as lever-type

✓ D-handles for drawers and cupboards

LIVING AND DINING AREAS

- Easy passage from kitchen to dining area
- Large enough to accommodate normal furnishings and provide adequate space for traffic
- Level floor with uniform surface texture
- Extra electrical outlets

✓ Extra electrical outlets

✓ Located conveniently close to a bathroom
✓ Sufficient room around a double bed for mobility

BEDROOMS

- One bedroom designed to be divided later
- Space on main living level designed as possible future bedroom
- Located conveniently close to a bathroom

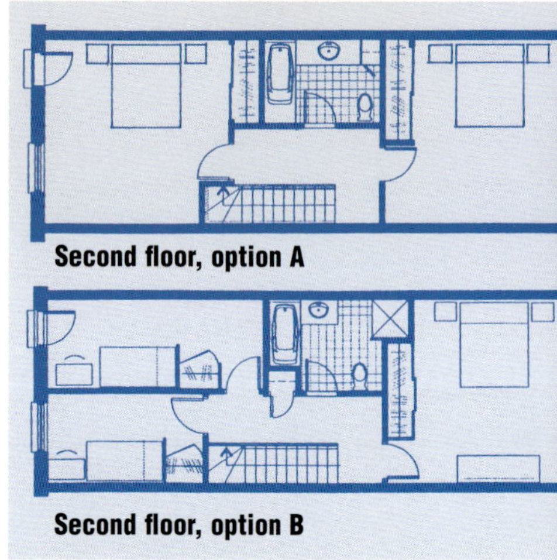

✓ One bedroom designed to be divided later

- Sufficient room around a double bed for mobility
- Switched outlets for light control and ceiling light
- Telephone and cable jack
- Closets with access from seated or standing position, adjustable rods and shelves

✓ Switched outlets for light control and ceiling light
✓ Telephone and cable jack

LAUNDRY FACILITIES

- Laundry area on the main or upper floor, close to the bathroom or bedrooms (if laundry is to be located initially in basement, provide easily adaptable space and electrical and plumbing connections for future relocation to the main floor)
- Appropriate task lighting
- Stacked front-loading washer and dryer with front controls

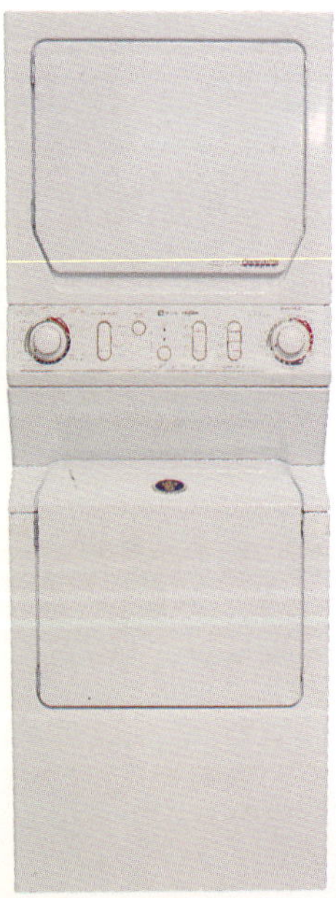

✓ Stacked front-loading washer and dryer with front controls

BALCONY

- Balcony floor level with the adjoining room
- Bevelled threshold no higher than 19 mm (¾ in.)
- Balcony enclosure that does not unduly restrict view from seated position
- Adequate lighting, switches inside
- Exterior electrical outlet

✓ Balcony floor level with the adjoining room
✓ Bevelled threshold no higher than 19 mm (¾ in.)
✓ Balcony enclosure that does not unduly restrict view from seated position

STORAGE SPACE

- Storage spaces and closets easily accessible for everyone
- Shelving and hanger rods with adjustable heights
- Light in storage space

WINDOWS

- Easily operated windows with cranks
- Sills not higher than 750 mm (30 in.) above floor level

✓ Easily operated windows with cranks
✓ Sills not higher than 750 mm (30 in.) above floor level

ELECTRICAL OUTLETS AND CONTROLS

- Electrical switches, outlets and mechanical system controls in easily accessible locations, reachable from both sitting and standing positions (1,200 mm [48 in.] for switches and 450 mm [18 in.]) for outlets
- Rocker-type light switches
- Circuit breaker panel located on main floor for easy access

✓ Rocker-type light switches

HEATING AND AIR CONDITIONING

- Heating system with easy access to central unit and controls
- Control of temperature by room or zone

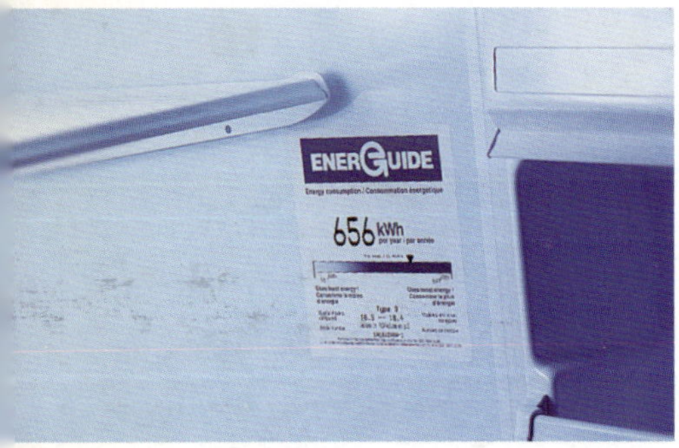

✓ Energy-efficient windows and appliances

HEALTHY HOUSING FEATURES

- Materials (wood, sealants, paints, drywall and insulation) with low emission of chemical vapours
- Energy-efficient windows and appliances
- Use of passive solar energy
- Rigid-board insulation
- Low-volume toilets and faucets

✓ Easy access to house, bevelled threshold 19 mm (¾ in.) high

✓ Non-slip paths and decks
✓ Level walkways with little or no slope

GARDEN

- Easy access to house, bevelled threshold 19 mm (¾ in.) high
- Non-slip paths and decks
- Level walkways with little or no slope